I've Got Cancer Where?

Janine McFarlane

Dedications

Supermum, without you, I honestly believe I would not have survived treatment. Thank you for your unlimited love and patience.

To my Nades, you continue to love me and forgive me for being the worst friend in the world, throughout this battle, you were my rock. Love you always chicken!

Last but most certainly not least, to my children, two of the most gorgeous, brilliant and interesting people I know, despite having me as a mother!

Contents

I've got Cancer where?

Introduction

First of all, I am no writer, throughout my school career many an English teacher would dismiss my efforts at creative writing as substandard and generally lacking. I tell you this to manage your expectations early, the contents of these pages are simply the story in my head, at times nonsensical and random, however this story is honest. In addition, I must apologise for the language, as I said, it is the thoughts in my head and many of those should be PG rated. On the 10th March 2017 with a single sentence my life changed, that sentence was "you have Cancer". To say this is a game changer is an understatement.

Now don't get me wrong, no Cancer is glamourous, however having to tell people you have ass cancer is slightly humiliating. Now it stands to reason that if I was to ever get a Cancer, Colon Cancer was always likely to be the one for me. Years of people telling me that I was full of shit and a pain in the ass eventually was to change from an opinion of my character to a physical reality. Nothing could have prepared me for what was to come. The following year proved to be incredibly challenging for my family and me.

I have throughout this book referred to this as a journey, aside from the obvious journey that is Cancer, it is a journey of self-discovery, one that has not been at all easy. While I talk a lot, I am generally not comfortable talking about how I feel, but I realised early on that I needed an outlet, somewhere to let my thoughts come out, so as with so many before me I decided to start a blog. This book is based on that blog. I started writing the blog with the thought that it may help anybody who has been diagnosed with Cancer and is currently going through the treatment, in the middle of treatment however I realised that it was likely to put the fear of God in anybody facing this journey.

I want to emphasise that everybody's experience is not the same, each person reacts differently to chemotherapy, my experience with it was unpleasant however that was my experience and that does not mean it would be the same for somebody else. This book may help family and loved one's who are supporting somebody going through treatment for Cancer, my hope is it can provide some clarity on how you feel when you are going through this. It is an extremely difficult time for those supporting a Cancer patient, some insight into what they are going through may be helpful.

Chapter 1

Where it all began …

There are a few reasons for the creation of this blog:

1. As a means of emptying out the clutter of my mind as it gets kind of noisy up there.

2. To keep anybody who is interested in my current news updated; and

3. To raise awareness about Colon Cancer, while historically a disease mostly found in folks in the latter stages of their lives, it is becoming more and more prevalent in the younger generation year on year. A piece of advice folks. listen to your body and ensure it gets the due care and attention it deserves when it is clearly telling you it needs help!

So, where did this all begin? I suggest the squeamish turn away now! In the early part of 2016, I had a rapid change in bowel movements, to summarise I went from being a regular once a day girl to needing to "go" between seven times on a good day to approximately fifteen times on a bad one. When I say "go", I don't mean "could do with finding a loo in the next half an hour or so", my body was giving me approximately 30 seconds to find the facilities before it was prepared to put me in a position which would be most undignified!

Obviously, this change was unsettling and while studying the contents of the loo are not generally a favoured pastime of mine, the fact that on each occasion the aftermath would resemble something from a scene of a mass murder was hard to miss. Naturally, this change sent off rather loud alarm bells and I swiftly arranged a visit to my local GP. I was given an appointment for a blood test and sent away with some sample containers to return the following day (when I say samples, I do not mean urine).

For anybody who has not had to provide a stool sample before, let me tell you – this creates some interesting challenges – our mothers taught us quite early on that playing with one's waste products was unsanitary and not socially acceptable so aside from the logistical challenges there is an internal conflict about the whole experience.I decided however that needs must and years of practical jokes i.e. the cling film over the toilet bowl suddenly became a rather useful idea as opposed to a means of making the midnight loo run of a mate rather entertaining.

I won't elaborate further but I got my sample and returned it to the surgery the next morning. The diagnosis received was that I had a Campylobacter infection caused by the poor handling of/consumption of raw poultry. From that day on my wonderful and loving partner, Steve became the chief in charge of all thing's poultry in the house as I refused to touch the stuff! Despite the treatment for the abovementioned bacteria being time and no dairy (no cheese, oh the torture!) a month passed by and the symptoms continued.

To say my current condition is restrictive does not even come close, you reach the point where leaving the house becomes a terrifying prospect and all activities are planned around where there are facilities that can be accessed post haste if needed. We won't cover the challenges faced by using public loos either, traumatic doesn't even cover it! Queue the next visit to the GP where I plonked myself down in the chair and said, "this needs sorting – I cannot carry on like this!". I was sent off again for more blood tests and you guessed it, a further stool sample was needed.

The results showed that the Campylobacter was gone and therefore the conclusion was that the cause was likely an inflammatory bowel disease, look up Ulcerative Colitis – the symptoms are identical to that of Colon Cancer. So, the treatment protocol for UC began, unfortunately this did not solve the problem either. Just a momentary rant, one would think that considering the frequency of bowel movements I would be losing weight by the hour – I am officially the only person who can go to the loo fifteen times a day and not lose a sodding gram!

Grumble over, but you must admit, there does seem to be some universal injustice being dished out here! Summer passed, during which we enjoyed two family camping trips to Cornwall, this is not a condition which is enjoyed in your own home so I can assure you at a campsite it is the stuff of nightmares! I reckon I could have left Usain Bolt in my wake with the speeds I reached when dashing to the toilet in the early hours of the morning! After this I decided that it was time to return to my GP and demand further attention.

My GP who we will refer to as Dr A, while as warm and fuzzy as a blanket made of steel wool; I do like his no-nonsense approach and he gets stuff done when he believes it is necessary. Even got the odd smile or two out of him due to my somewhat inappropriate sense of humour regarding my current situation. Dr A referred me to Gastroenterology for further exploration, unfortunately with the demand on the NHS being what it is the first appointment was in May 2017, bear in mind we are still in August 2016 at this point.

I would like to clarify at this stage that this is not a criticism of the NHS, I find the system to be full of dedicated, hardworking individuals who are stretched to breaking point without the resources to deliver the service required of a those in the profession of healing. Bless you all, your commitment amazes me daily! As luck would have it my appointment was brought forward to February and at 9am on Saturday the 25th February I got to meet my GI Doc.

After an interrogation of my symptoms and a cursory inspection of my abdominal region he suggested I attend the Endoscopy unit for a Colonoscopy, further elaboration on this delightful procedure later! I went for more blood tests and of course, the opportunity to study yet more of my poo (snigger snigger, I said poo!) is never to be missed. At this point I was beginning to question whether the cling film should remain in the kitchen or become a permanent addition to the medical cabinet?! At this appointment I was also given a box which resembled the same type in which you receive a new and shiny mobile phone, alas the contents were not as exciting. The box contained Moviprep which is a laxative capable of shifting concrete!

The Thursday night before the procedure was spent drinking two litres of what can only be described as the culinary equivalent of lemon flavoured craft glue, this is to be consumed with a further two litres of water, somebody please pass me the barf bucket! What follows is not worth getting into, let's just say I felt extremely clean by the following morning!

I arrived for the procedure and was given a sedative; I was not so much worried about the pain but decided to be slightly "out of it" might make the indignity of the procedure less scarring! In short, imagine a length of hosepipe with a camera attached being maneuvered around your insides through the old back passage! Involuntary shudder commences now. While watching my insides on the screen (this does not make for attractive viewing by the way!) the camera came across something that could only be described as alien and deeply unattractive, we are talking Jabba the Hutt kind of ugly! The audience behind me grew and there were hushed whispers of biopsies and taking markers. Being of reasonable intelligence I was aware I was not looking at something that could be treated with an antibiotic and lots of fluids. Damn!

I was then wheeled off to a cubicle and a nurse was sent off to locate my partner Steve who was off topping up the parking ticket. Once located he was brought into the cubicle where the words "tumour and cancerous" were all I remembered hearing. He did say however that most cases are "operable and curable", unfortunately what Steve heard was "inoperable and incurable", I do believe he lost 5 years of his life at that moment but the lovely Doctor repeated his statement and so Steve was able to breathe again. Having had an experience once before where your whole life is changed in an instant I felt better equipped to handle this.

So far to date there has been no panic, major tears or drama, simply the realisation of "manage each day/challenge as it comes – don't borrow problems that may never become a reality!" We are two weeks into the journey and are truthfully none the wiser about what the future holds, I have a team working in the background on formulating the best treatment plan for me and until given cause to consider otherwise will have faith in them to take care of me. I am not afraid, this is just another one of life's challenges sent to test me, while I have sometimes taken the wrong path but ultimately, I have overcome these hurdles eventually and come out stronger for it and intend to do the same with this one. The hardest part of this for me has been the angst of my family and loved ones, I understand their fear and were I in their position would likely be a jibbering idiot by now. I will keep you updated as to my progress and promise to continue boring you with my wordy ramblings. I know that most of you got bored halfway through and switched over to YouTube to watch cute puppy videos! To close I thought I would share with you one of my favourite jokes, while funny there is a lot of truth in this, take note!

All the organs of the body were having a meeting, trying to decide who was the one in charge.

"I should be in charge," said the brain, "Because I run all the body's systems, so without me nothing would happen."

"I should be in charge," said the blood, "because I circulate oxygen all over so without me you'd all waste away."
"I should be in charge," said the stomach, "because I process food and give all of you energy."

"I should be in charge," said the legs, "because I carry the body wherever it needs to go."

"I should be in charge," said the eyes, "Because I allow the body to see where it goes."

"I should be in charge," said the rectum, "Because I'm responsible for waste removal."

All the other body parts laughed at the rectum and insulted him, so in a huff, he shut down tight.

Within a few days, the brain had a terrible headache, the stomach was bloated, the legs got wobbly, the eyes got watery, and the blood was toxic. They all decided that the rectum should be the boss.

The Moral of the story?   The ass hole is usually in charge!

Chapter 2

A bit of background

Alas we have no more news, I am booked in for an MRI in the morning and unfortunately this means we will only have further information after next week Wednesday as the results won't be back in time for the Multi-Disciplinary Meeting this week. Well, no point in grumbling – might as well continue to get on with the business of living! I thought with the absence of further information on my cancer situation I would indulge myself in a little more literary therapy and provide some information on my life to date as well as give you some background on some of my important people as to date you are only aware of my Steve. The reason for this is simply because I have had an overwhelming response to my first blog and there are many who are now reading it who don't know me as intimately as my original target audience.

Yesterday was Mother's Day, being a Mum is probably the greatest gift I have ever had, and equally natures greatest prank on humanity – the fact that my genes were thrown into some biological lottery and the breath holding by the universe was not "am I going to win millions" but rather "Oh my God, surely mother nature won't inflict yet another one of these onto humankind? As it turns out Mother Nature is a wicked old girl who likes to take a bit of a gamble!) I appreciate I am biased, but I believe that my two sons are quite possibly the most amazing and unique individuals ever to grace this planet.

My eldest, Brett is deeply intelligent, gorgeous and thankfully the vast majority of his nature he gets from his Dad. This child is one of the most talented musicians one could ever encounter, what he can do with a guitar is nothing short of magical. My youngest son is a lot like his Mum, I often look at him and predict that the next 20 or so years of his life will be an obstacle course filled with extreme highs and equally the same depth in lows, very often of his own making. Words from one who shares your character my love – this makes for an adventure which is to be enjoyed to the maximum with a few scars collected on the way.

The reason these thoughts came into my head tonight was because as parents we are often faced with being responsible for navigating our children through the good and the bad, both my boys have had to deal with situations at an early age that most of us who have passed some of the big milestone birthdays thankfully have not. I could ask myself why and curse the universe for not allowing my boys to have a childhood unmarred by tragedy and sadness but then what would be the point, life happens to all of us and my darling children who I would give anything to be able to shield from hurt and worry are no exception. One can only hope they choose the path whereby they recognise that to truly appreciate joy you need to have felt the other end of the emotional spectrum.

As mentioned in episode one of this blog, I am no stranger to life changing experiences, at the age of 27 I received a phone call at 2:55am on the 31st August that changed my life forever (precise I know but the image of that time showing on the clock when the phone woke me will forever be burned into my brain). The voice on the other end of the phone was my brother-in-law, Laurence asking if my husband Adam was home, I replied that he was still out after celebrating the birthday of a friend and had not returned home yet. Laurence's words like the time on the clock will too forever be included on the "notable memory" shelf in my head, "J, there has been an accident, we are coming to pick you up".

In the car with Adam was a very dear friend Cameron, so we went to pick up his partner, Nadine, (somebody who deserves more than a minor part in this blog but will return to Nadine later). Halfway to my Parents-in-law we got the phone call that we were all praying would never come, Adam & Cameron were both killed in the accident. From this point on much of the following year becomes a blur, there are snippets I can recall but I have learnt that the human mind is a spectacular piece of kit – it protects you from anything too painful to recall. One of the snippets I remember and will never forget was sitting on the settee with my 7-year-old son and telling him that his Dad was never coming back, nothing can prepare you on how to deliver that message. Having worked in HR for many years and being asked the question "how do you deliver bad news to people all the time", my answer "when you have delivered news like I had to deliver on that fateful August day to the most precious human being in my world, nothing is ever that hard again!".

Life however has a way of proving you wrong, there was a message that proved equally hard to deliver and again, to my most precious of audiences, my children and that message was "I have cancer! However, unlike the first message this is one that is not so cruel and final – this one I plan to ensure has a happy ending. Having shared with you this rather momentous event in my 42 years it would be remiss not to share the memory of this beautiful man the world lost, Adam was truly one of life's last gentleman, he had a smile so warm that was matched equally by the warmth of his heart. There is a view that when people die we put them on a pedestal, for Adam there was no need, he was at the tender age of 27 one of the most wonderful people I have ever known, I all too often secretly questioned whether he was too good for me and many times the reply to this question was "probably". I only hope that even though during our time together I was a bit of a horror (and I was) he is looking down on me now saying "you did good chicken!".

While I will never say that losing Adam had a silver lining as the sun has shone a little less brightly since he left us I will say this tragic event marked an all-important crossroad in my life where I had to make a choice, the path of the victim or that to becoming the strong woman we all aspire to be. I would love to say I instantly chose the path of success but that would be a bloody lie, I spent the following years making some horrendous choices involving some particularly bad behaviour! I believe it was inevitable, to say I was a wild child is the understatement of the century – the details of my misadventures will be excluded from this blog as this is a family programme and my children are watching!

However, it was on this path of self-destruction I met Duncan, aka Grumpy! Grumpy was the man who entered the space previously filled by Adam and I can honestly say was largely responsible for saving my life and setting me on the straight and narrow resulting in the person I am today. Our relationship was not to last but from it I got the gift of my beautiful youngest son and in Grumpy somebody who I still and will always consider to be one of my dearest friends in the whole world!

Through Duncan I was introduced to Cheryl who is one of my heroes, she became my boss, my mentor and a very dear friend. Cheryl took what was a broken woman with a chip on her shoulder the size of Everest and over the course of only a few years through support and guidance put me back on track. Cheryl is and will always be my greatest inspiration and without whom I believe I would have become a deeply unpleasant individual. Worth noting, Cheryl is a 3-time big C survivor, the woman is a legend! For now, and always Cheryl, thank you for believing in me when I didn't, I owe you so much more than you will ever know (or acknowledge).

Through Cheryl I entered the world of HR, holy cow, never believe this to be a dull job … many grey hairs but SO many rewarding experiences, somebody in the profession said to me once "get out while you still can, the job is soul destroying. I must say I disagree, like anything in life HR is what you make of it, you have the means to provide the opportunity for people to realise their full potential and watch them grow. Having seen this so many times I can tell you it is so incredibly rewarding, I cannot take the credit for their success – all I did was provide the platform and they grasped the opportunity, put in the hard work and flew. I salute you all!

I mentioned my darling Nadine, or Nades as she shall from henceforth be referred to. So Nades was a dear friend before our shared tragedy of becoming widowed so early in life however due to this experience she was to become somebody so central to my world that nothing will ever shift her from it (not even Moviprep!) Nadine is the most incredible friend, to me and so many others – she fondly (we are going to assume fondly …) refers to me as her "best worst friend ever".

To clarify why, if there was an appraisal conducted measuring my success rating as a friend, I reckon I would sit firmly in the "Below Expectations" bracket. I am terrible at keeping in touch, I am so wrapped up in my own world/job/latest hobby that I have been known to go underground for months (maybe years) on end only to emerge and expect people to be there where I left them.

Nadine always is, she does however admonish me on a regular basis for this behaviour but nevertheless is always there. This is a woman who never so much as ran for the bus but then blew us all away by taking up running and successfully completing the London Marathon, she will hate me for this but for those of you who have watched Toy Story, Nadine's running style is very similar to that of Rex the dinosaur – something to behold I tell you.

To close off the introduction of Nadine however I want to give you a snapshot of who she is as a person, some years back Nades had a friend who also sadly was diagnosed with aggressive Breast Cancer, Nades was on her wedding day sporting a head of beautiful long locks which the day after her wedding she had chopped off to donate to the cause of making wigs for cancer patients in honour of her friend. In support of a friend Nades went from Rapunzel to GI Jane, who wouldn't want this woman in their corner?

Footnote, Nades has declared to give up sugar and all things nice in support of my current condition, although she has declared Whisky is off the table as it offers medicinal value during this time of great stress.

In every drama there needs to be those people there to provide you with some comic relief, those people who are there that make you forget your woes for a moment simply by being who they are, enter onto the stage two people who have in a relatively short time become exceptionally important to me, Cecil (not his real name but that by which he goes in our home) and his beautiful other half, our very own Polish Princess, Kasia. On being diagnosed you go through the inevitable motions of telling your nearest and dearest and Cecil and Kasia were at the top of the list, we skyped them on the Saturday after we got the news and I spent 1.5 hours laughing until the tears were rolling down my face, on recently being told some of the worst news you could ever receive believe me laughter is the best therapy there is. With these two we get hours and hours of therapy that if you had to put a value to it would be the equivalent of my years' salary, but in fact the true value of their friendship is priceless.

The mums in my corner, these two women could take down an army of Gladiators with their sheer strength and determination! Steve's Mum, Pauline; a more passionate woman I have yet to meet, I believe if she were to enter 10 Downing Street and oversee all national policy and reform that Britain would truly be great again, this is someone who doesn't suffer fools and it is only fair to pass a warning for those responsible for my care, get it right or heaven help you!! I don't want you to get the impression Pauline is a tyrant, not at all, this is a woman who is loving and warm and cares for her family above all else.

My Mum, so much to say but there are not enough words to convey what this woman means to me. A beautiful woman, inside and out, my Mum would give up her last penny to anybody who she thought needed it more (she has in fact done this in the past!) Through my many trials and tribulations my Mum has been my strength when I had none left, she has been my safety net when I have fallen and helped put me back together when I was broken (temptation to refer to Humpty Dumpty and the many similarities we share but don't want to spoil the moment). My Mum truly puts her children and grandchildren before herself without ever asking for anything in return. I am not afraid of cancer because I know that with her by my side there is nothing I cannot face.

Steve, he has been mentioned but it is only fair to give you an idea of who this man is. The past year has been physically and mentally rather trying for me, because of my symptoms I have been in a lot of pain and rather anaemic which has left me just short of useless, Steve has taken on the burden of managing most of the household tasks without complaint when I have not been capable. On diagnosis I had an impulse not unlike that which expectant mums go through, which was the overwhelming urge to "nest"! I decided that on top of everything else now was to time to redecorate the lounge, Steve has supported this badly timed whim and is wholeheartedly tackling the project and is hard at work as we speak. I count my lucky stars every day that this man came into my life. I look forward to our retirement which at this stage involves a motorhome and a trike, destination anywhere!

Finally, there is one being that cannot escape mention, this would be our precious fur baby Dave! He gets the full name treatment as he is unlikely to object to being named on the net, Dave is a 55kg Bernese Mountain Dog who is the centre of our household. All you doggy types out there will understand the gravity of the love you can feel for your canine companion, this boy is a constant source of love and joy in my life and he will be an important part of my healing as puppy cuddles are widely recognised as having great therapeutic value.

While there are SO many other people who will be making up my army over the next few months and I don't wish for any of you who have not been mentioned that you are any less loved, those who have received a mention here are simply the generals who will be leading me into battle however this does not make the contribution of the rest of my clan any less needed or valuable. I love you all and thank you for your thoughts and prayers. I appreciate this update is rather deep and serious, so unlike me I know but promise that hereafter I will revert to the person you all know and some even like as "serious Sally" is not a facade that suits me.

A photo of myself with the beautiful Dave taken in Wales.

I've got Cancer where?

Chapter 3

The verdict is in!

Phew … the past few weeks have been a test of our strength I tell you! So many people who are members of this club have emphatically stated, "the waiting to find out exactly what stage you are at is the worst part", they know what they are talking about, it has been tough! We have spent the past few weeks muddling through life as best we know how, Steve by donning his toolbelt and turning our living room from 70's chic into a space deserving of a slot on Grand Designs. The man is a legend!

I on the other hand have simply continued to live as though there is nothing amiss in my perfect world and while on the surface all has appeared well, by the end of week 3 my body decided it was time to demonstrate the physiological effects of not acknowledging stress. Of course, the area most prone to reacting to inner turmoil is the old gut, it is no coincidence that the saying when one has a traumatic experience is "I nearly crapped myself!". Being the area of my body currently causing me the issues which culminated in the creation of this blog, by week 4 I was in a lot of pain and not a happy bunny.

However, I don't believe there is a right or wrong way to get through this phase, you just have to do what feels right for you! Anyway, back to the important stuff. I met with my surgeon on Thursday to get my results, what a lovely man! Instantly felt comfortable that this was the man for the job. My Cancer is a Stage 3, as it has grown through the bowel wall and has crept its way into some of the lymph nodes. However, I have discovered that of all the cancers mine is a rather lazy one, the Doc reckons this little bugger may have been growing for as much as 15 years! 15 years and it is the size of a grape! I shit you not, the little bastard is a measly 3cm across.

I am extremely grateful for the sloth like characteristics of this thing I feel lucky that of all the cancers I could have got, I got the one that is always going to be the last to be picked to join teams in PE by his classmates! Which leads me to my point, although a Stage 3 it is not aggressive which means we can destroy the little sod without fear of it suddenly dashing off to attach itself to some other distant organ.

The lovely surgeon is confident we are going to sort it out swiftly and without too much fuss. It is interesting however that due to my age the cause behind this is likely to be genetic as this is a cancer generally considered to be a disease of the elderly and while becoming more prevalent in the young is still quite rare. I will be tested by a genetics team to establish if this is the case which will be quite interesting and always one to find the silver lining, if I do have this faulty gene then it provides my family with a head start as they can be tested and if the genetic markers are found in their makeup they can start getting regular screening done which will catch any nasties early. Y'all can thank me in the form of cash gifts or holidays!! Lovely surgeon said that as I am young … YES, HE SAID YOUNG!!! LOVE THE MAN ALREADY!

Anyway, I digress, as I am young, they will be treating the invasive little shit quite aggressively… 5 weeks of radiotherapy and chemotherapy followed by surgery to remove the nasty nodule then followed by more chemo. I don't foresee this period being a time of sunshine and rainbows, but needs must and as my new favourite quote goes, "Life isn't about waiting for the storm to pass, it's learning to dance in the rain!" I intend to do the Charleston while leaping from puddle to puddle, got a good pair of wellies at the ready!

One thing that will be interesting is after surgery I will have a temporary colostomy bag for six months to give my bowel a chance to heal. For those of you not in the know about these things, I will have a bag attached to my intestine through my stomach to collect … ahem … waste! (go on, get the eeeeeewwwwwww bit out the way before we continue …) While I am sure this will no doubt present some challenges, one must make the best of it and I have already found some wicked bag covers, my favourite being one with "Shit happens" printed on it. Lovin' it!! My son is horrified at my delight at what is available and is already thinking of reasons not to be seen with me in public for fear I may be inclined to show my newest accessories off.

That is, you all caught up on the cancer stuff, I will do regular updates about where we are and how things are going as we move through the above phases. Before I close off this post I feel it would be remiss not to share something quite special we were part of tonight, the dashing, charming and all round great guy, Cecil (if I didn't put that in I would not have heard the bloody end of it) got down on one knee and proposed to our beautiful Polish Princess whilst surrounded by friends and family, oh and we were invited too! It was truly wonderful to share this moment with this fantastic couple and it provided a further reminder that there are so many joys left to fight for, a wedding somewhere in the Caribbean being one of them. Big love and congratulations both. Until next time, keep dancing in the rain .

Chapter 4

My first "meh" post!

I have allowed myself this moment to have a mini moan, for a couple of reasons:

- My family don't have to be the only audience for my moaning (poor S, the man has the patience of a Saint).

- Bottling up misery is toxic and needs to be released, I am the patient on the couch, and you are all holding the role of therapists patiently listening to my whining … sorry, appreciate you are not being paid accordingly;

- I don't want to pretend that this journey is nothing but an exercise in positive thinking – there are elements that royally suck and to pretend otherwise is a farce.

Since I received my diagnosis I feel like my world has spiralled completely out of control, I accept that we never truly have total control of our lives but the little I did have I feel has been lost to me completely.

My job which is extremely important to me is no longer something I can do, due to the escalation of my symptoms over the past few weeks I am no longer able to get up in the morning and go to work. I have left my amazing team with little warning or support and simply abandoned ship. I hate this more than you could imagine as I feel I am letting my team and company down. My company has been unbelievably good to me, and I hate to just leave them during a time where they need all hands-on deck. I miss my colleagues, they are not only the people I work with, they are my friends, my family and my support system.

My routine, my world has gone from the typical 9 – 5, Monday to Friday followed by weekends chilling out as we see fit to never ending Hospital appointments. I miss the mundane routines, I miss doing housework, I miss Monday mornings!!! My body, it no longer makes any sense to me – recent blood tests show severe anaemia, I am potentially facing a blood transfusion.

I have days where I can barely lift my head from the pillow, walking up the stairs leaves me breathless and feeling like my heart is about to burst out of my chest. I feel like a 40 a day girl now! With little warning I can go from feeling reasonably normal to being doubled over to the point where I am throwing up rather violently due to the pain, it is like watching a scene from The Exorcist. Thank heavens my darling Mum arrived on Sunday and is forever nearby armed with the necessary equipment to minimise the damage of these unfortunate episodes.

Not only is she looking after me but counselling my precious pup who finds these moments rather upsetting and becomes rather fretful – it is a scene to behold, Mum passing me the puke bucket, rubbing my back and gently shushing Dave to try calm him down. Without her I would be lost!

Most of all I miss my patience, while generally not a very patient individual I have honed the craft of being patient with people over the years, I am proud of the fact that I have become more tolerant and understanding and believe this has made me better at my job. The past few weeks have seen my hard work fly out the window and I am finding it very hard to remain patient at all. I know this is down to the fact that my life no longer feels like it is my own, I feel like it is co-owned by this hideous disease and the NHS and this is making me grumpy.

This is lack of patience is mostly at people closest to me, people care and do so by questioning me on and sharing their views about my choices and decisions – this is not sitting well and I am forced to bite my tongue and smile but I fear the day the demon is released and some poor unsuspecting soul gets their head ripped off. May I apologise in advance if it is any of you … Forgiven??

I feel like my world will never be the same again, I have a battle on my hands to beat this little bastard and I fully intend to do so. As mentioned in my previous post the opinion of my medical team is the cause of this is genetic, so feel like my body is a time bomb and this may not be the only time I am faced with this battle. I feel like I am being stalked by the Grim Reaper, like the sneaky little bastard is spying on me sniggering to himself while rubbing his bony mitts together. I will no doubt find my way through this fog and remove this cloak of doom which has descended over recent days. I am sorry you have had to sit and listen to my woes but feel it is important to be honest about all of this, to pretend my world is nothing but unicorns and rainbows would be a lie and equally disrespectful to those who travel this rocky path with me.

Hopefully tomorrow will be a brighter day and I will wake up full of the joys of Spring. Until next time, thanks for all the love, support and understanding – it means the world to me and is what will get me through this.

Chapter 5

Slowly does it!

We have all watched Grey's Anatomy and the like where upon diagnosis of Cancer the patient is whisked off and instantly hooked up with the necessary treatment and everything happens in lightning fast time. I suppose this is essential when their story must be covered in 45 minutes. In the real world of a Cancer patient this is not the case, the days, weeks and months post diagnosis involves what feels like endless waiting. Waiting for the next letter for the next appointment which is followed by yet another wait for another letter for another appointment.

This has been my life for the past 5 weeks. There is no rush, no panic, it is all a process to be followed to the letter. For many I can imagine this would be unnerving as when you hear the words "you have Cancer" all you want is to have this thing out of you.

I however have found this lack of frenzied activity to be quite calming, there is no immediate concern that my body is going to fail me unless something is done today, we have time to prepare me for what is coming, time to bolster up the various bodily functions to ensure that when I start my treatment I am ready for it.

Many around me don't see it that way and want everything to happen now, but we all need to remember I am one of thousands currently in this place and we are all equally deserving of a slot in the busy schedules of the professionals responsible for our care. Today at another appointment I got to see the brave faces of some of those people, sitting in the waiting room surrounded by men and women who are undergoing treatment, they are obviously suffering, the pain is written on their faces and yet they continue to smile, share a joke with their companions and greeting the Nurses as though old friends. The world is full of heroes, my fellow cancer sufferers are now mine. This is true strength in the face of adversity!

I met my Oncologist today, we shall call him Dr V. I have so much admiration for anybody who chooses to enter this field, your days are spent delivering news and information which could be the most upsetting and terrifying the person sitting opposite you is likely to ever hear. To do this and remain positive must take some doing, hats off to them!

Back to Dr V … he is so like my GP Dr A, unlikely to be everybody's cup of tea, rather monotone and there is a slim chance he will ever be asked to play Santa Claus for any community Christmas events but he is right up my alley. He was very thorough and talked me through my scans which was very informative and strangely interesting. The thing however that clinched the deal for me was the discovery that Dr V has a sense of humour akin to my own, on discussing my country of origin being South Africa and the ongoing troubles with the current leader his suggested solution was "why don't they just shoot the bastard?" Yup, it was that moment that cemented our relationship, many think these thoughts, but my favourite people are those who just come out and say it.

I now understand the reason behind the pain and discomfort, my tumour while theoretically small is not a single lump but has in fact grown around the inner lining of the colon making that section extremely thin, some basic maths, the section of the colon it is in has an average diameter of 5cm, my tumour is 3 cm wide. Large rare steaks are a thing of the past for me as anything that is difficult to digest stops the works completely and it backs up in there as fast as the M25 on a bank holiday weekend. Any further meals thereafter come straight back out via the original entry point. Yuck!!!!

This coupled with the fact that based on the images on the scan my Uterus is trying to take over the world!! My poor bladder is currently the kid with his face being squished up against the window of the overcrowded bus so never mind it having the space to hold any fluid it hardly has room just to fit in, it seems my frequent potty runs for a pee are not down to my increasing years but to an issue with real estate in there! All the above makes my pelvic area a scene like that on a tube in London rush hour, lots of pushing and shoving, this constant activity makes for ongoing discomfort as all these internal organs are fighting for position and getting bruised and battered in the process, not fun – thank you to the pharmaceutical company who invented Tramadol!

My next steps are to go in for a further CT scan to plot the course for my Radiotherapy, yup, another letter for another appointment. I also have to meet with the Chemo team who will talk me through the Chemo and what to expect. So, in a nutshell we are still going through the motions and there is no starting date for the treatment, but we are getting there, slowly but surely.

As one of the reasons for this blog is to educate people on this journey, I would like to take a moment to share an observation and offer some advice. As mentioned at the start of this post this journey is slow and may not move at a pace that is deemed acceptable to all. If you are supporting someone going through this, getting frustrated at the system and ranting at the person about the lack of progress is not helpful. We are already going through enough, we need all our energy for this fight, be supportive, be positive and remain calm. If you are angry and want to shout and scream do so out of earshot, punch the wall, kick the door but when you are around us smile and offer a cup of tea. This is what we need from you now. Thanks for listening, will be back soon x

I've got Cancer where?

Chapter 6

Cancer guilt …

I have met quite a few of my fellow "cancer club members" over recent weeks, when I say met naturally, I mean online, that's where all the cool kids hang out these days isn't it? Our club members come in all shapes, sizes, colours and range in age from those who have not yet started driving to those who proudly sport a free bus pass, between us there are many differences but the most important shared characteristic is the one that bonds us, we have cancer … bummer!

The reason for the title of this post is not because I personally am suffering from some type of guilt that I may have caused this disease, in my humble opinion guilt is a wasted emotion, it takes up time, energy and headspace best reserved for that on which you can effect change, the past you cannot – it is gone! However, many of my fellow club members are suffering from severe feelings of guilt, the frequent cries heard are "I smoked, drank or ate too much". This makes me so sad, as we embark on the battle of a lifetime to punish yourself even further seems just too cruel!

My view – I love life, I live it and thoroughly enjoy all the delights it has to offer, most of the time to excess. Food and I have had a long and loving relationship, I am particularly fond of the type filled with sugar and heart stopping amounts of saturated fat. Size 10 jeans are such a fond but distant memory... I have also been known to enjoy a Tequila or twelve on a night out with mates resulting in the mother of all hangovers, but not to be put off I will gladly repeat this tomfoolery again on the next occasion to prove I can still hold my own.

Although I avoid using words like tomfoolery during these outings as to use this type of language severely damages one's street cred! There is a point to my waffle believe it or not, could I sit here and beat myself up for not taking better care of myself? Absolutely! Could I tell myself that my irresponsible ways have caused this cancer? For sure! But will I? Hell no!!

If my life had to end tomorrow is there a single thing I regret? No there isn't ... I have never regretted any of it and certainly won't start now. Is this disease caused by bad genes, poor diet choices, who knows? Why spend our precious time interrogating our lives? It won't make the cancer go away; you will simply add more stress to an already stressful situation. To all my fellow friends in battle, fight the disease, not yourself.

Let the Doctors and Cancer Research teams figure out the "why" about cancer, that is their job, your job is to take care of the most important person on this journey, YOU! As for me I continue to live as I always have, life is great, and I love it. I may feel decidedly crap most of the time but this only makes you appreciate the good days when the pain is at a minimum, the sun is shining and you are surrounded by the people you love, today was one those days and it was glorious! Have a great week y'all!

I've got Cancer where?

Chapter 7

I got inked!

Sorry to disappoint, I never had a cancer crisis moment and booked in to have a full back piece done, while a tattoo is on my bucket list I have commitment issues and a fear of permanent body markings, but hey, now that I have 3 of the most pathetic tats ever I may just suck it up at the end of my treatment and finally take the plunge!

Worth mentioning, aside from being a commitment phobe I am not a great fan of pain either (oh how much fun am I going to have over the next few months??) So, my other thinking is this, post colostomy reversal there may be some nerve damage resulting in numbness therefore creating the perfect canvas for my new addition, this way I can sit there and file my nails while being shot with needles and look well cool!!! My plan may be flawed but it works in my head. The explanation behind my pathetic body art for those of you who's world has not been touched by this horrid disease as follows, for Radiotherapy you need to have marks tattooed to be able to line up the laser thingies on specific points of your body for the zappy bit to hit the right spot i.e. the tumour.

In my case I have 3, one on each hip and one in the centre of my pelvic region. This is some seriously clever technology I tell you, you get a CT scan done which builds an image of the tumour which is then fed into the radiotherapy machine so the treatment is targeted to only zap the actual tumour which minimises the damage to the surrounding good tissue, kind of like a reverse 3D printer.I had my scan taken this week, I went in and met the Radiography team doing my scans, for a moment I thought it was bring your kid to work day", the sweet young chap introduced himself as Tim and then talked me through the treatment, he did it well but I was still convinced he spent his breaks watching Teletubby reruns!!!

The second Radiographer who joined Tim to do my scan was no older, it was at this point that it dawned on me that they were not young, I am just getting bloody old! Now nothing to date about this process is dignified or sexy, let's take a moment to discuss hospital gowns … do they tie in the front? The back? Why do some have 3 armholes, are we expecting health tourism to be undertaken by some intergalactic visitors? Bloody Nora, each encounter with the dreaded gown is exhausting, and this doesn't even cover the delicate issue of having your rear hanging out for all the world to see, note to hospital gown manufacturers "some of us are tall, larger than a size 6 and to whom gravity has come a calling!! Please be a bit more generous, I estimate providing us our dignity by adding on a few extra inches of fabric will cost you a maximum of about 20p per gown!

So, we are now at the stage where 90% of the prep work is done and now we just wait for the letter inviting us to the meeting to discuss dates, Yup, we continue to play the letter and meeting game, SO BORED NOW!! As for me personally, mentally I am holding up well, my physical state continues to be a challenge but not unmanageable. My support crew in the form of Steve and Supermum are taking truly awesome care of me. My Mum has just taken over and is truly being an absolute star, the irony is I am the most ill I have ever been but through her careful management of my nutritional needs I am the healthiest I have been in years, a contradiction I know but it is true.

My body will be ready to face the treatment purely down to the excellent care I am receiving. In addition to this she is doing all the chores assisted by Steve and won't let me lift a finger. In between all this ensuring my hot water bottles are always toasty. I am so lucky to have her and can never thank her enough for everything. I do not know how I would have coped without her. Enough prattling on from me, till next time, take care and keep smiling.

I've got Cancer where?

Chapter 8

Feeling a little green …

As you are all now aware, I have bowel cancer, for the past decade or so this nasty little so and so has been slowly trying to destroy me from the inside and whilst slow has been incredibly successful in its mission! I have been extremely ill and didn't realise how bad things were getting, if one refers to the story about the boiling frog, this was most definitely the case with me. When you wake up one morning with a cold you know you are sick, when the deterioration happens over the period of years it just feels normal.

Enter Supermum and her team of loyal friends who hail from the world of Naturopathic medicine. Now before you are doubting Delilah's all start muttering things like "snake oil and tree huggers" give me a chance, I too was like you. In fact, I was probably the leader of the pack! How can some supplements and changing your diet help you when you have advanced cancer … pah, stuff and nonsense!! Or is it … see exhibit no. 1 below, a photo of me taken just before

Supermum arrived to take charge of my care followed by a photo taken 5 weeks later. Lordy, I was an unattractive beastie, just missing my prison number! My poor body was failing, badly! Although you cannot see it in this photo, my skin is a lovely shade of yellow, my liver was about ready to break up with me and go find a life partner more deserving! Sorry Liv!!

And then we have the photo taken 5 weeks later, I would like to state for the record that neither Photoshop nor Plastic Surgeons were used in the process. This transformation is purely down to a change in my diet and a carefully planned protocol of supplements.

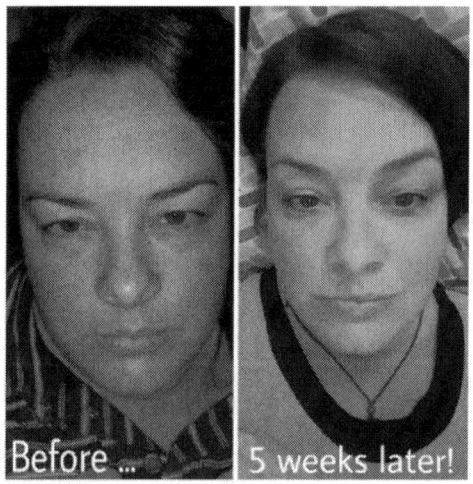

Before any of you good folk ask, there is little point in me sharing my plan as this programme is very specifically tailored to suit the individual. The change you see on the outside I can assure you is nothing compared to what I feel like on the inside, I feel incredible, I have not felt this well for years! My symptoms are under control for the most part, pain is at a minimum and I have loads of energy. As I have repeatedly said to Supermum, in the state I was in I doubt I could have survived the treatment, never mind the disease. I am now a massive advocate for the field of Natural Medicine, yup folks, me – the Tequila chugging frequent flyer of McDonald's.

Who would have thought it! Let's not kid ourselves, there will always be that slice of cheesecake that is too enticing to refuse but as with everything in life it is all about balance. I start my treatment tomorrow and I am ready for it, I realise now the importance of taking care of myself will be the difference between surviving and not. I plan to be around raising hell for many more years so bring on the green stuff!!

I've got Cancer where?

Chapter 9

What's it like to have cancer?

I read somewhere once that you will never understand what it is like to have cancer until you have cancer … seems logical yes? I never really understood the depth of this statement until … yup, you guessed it … I got bloody cancer!!! It is all consuming, it takes over your body, mind and life. Your every thought centres on surviving this thing and coming out on the other side with your sanity intact (I appreciate in my case to claim the presence of total sanity is probably a stretch but would like to try hang on to the shred I had!)

Two years ago, almost to the day I started treatment, Steve and I were enjoying the holiday of a lifetime in the Maldives. We were diving some of the best reefs our oceans have to offer, spending hours lounging in the sun sipping delicious rum cocktails without a care in the world. A year after the Maldives holiday Steve and I bought our first home together and soon after expanded our family by welcoming our much-adored fur baby Dave. I would so often sit and reflect on how lucky I was, I had everything I could ever wish for, life was perfect …

Today life is filled with pain, fear and uncertainty. I am strong and will face whatever comes, but there are times I get angry. Nobody deserves this so will never ask "why me?" I mean why not me. But I will ask "why now?" I want to be planning family holidays, deciding on paint colours, bitching because my fat ass won't get into my Summer clothes and vowing that Monday I will start my diet in earnest (only to be defeated on Tuesday by the presence of birthday doughnuts at the office!)

We cancer sufferers can all deny that the dark thoughts exist, but we are only lying to ourselves. There is the constant terror which exists somewhere deep down inside, it is not death that scares me but the effect it would have on my friends and family. I don't want to be the cause of any more pain in their lives than I am now. I fear being told "there is nothing more we can do" and then having to wait for "the end". I would like to think I would make the most of that time and enjoy it and not become consumed by anger and resentment but there is no telling! Please don't think for one second this is me being negative and admitting defeat, I am simply sharing the thoughts that keep me awake some nights. On the 10th March 2017 my life changed forever and will never be the same again. I read the saying somewhere that "to spend the rest of your life worrying about cancer is to waste the rest of your life".

Very profound but suggest this may have been written by someone who has never had cancer! Short of a nice neat dose of selective amnesia I am not sure this is completely achievable!

Every day I go for treatment and consider the faces of my fellow patients and while many of us remain upbeat and smile outwardly we see the pain and fear in each other's eyes. Will this look leave if we are lucky enough to be declared to be disease free? I would like to believe so but am not too sure. For now, I accept that it is what it is and I have no choice but to get on with it, my treatment is going well, I have bad days where the pain is almost too much to bear but then I also have great days where I am pain free and these days are thankfully in the majority.

So far chemo has been kind (although will save my cries of hallelujah as it is early days yet so won't break out the bubbly just yet), I am little nauseous and much to the horror of Supermum I could rival the pickiest toddler when it comes to food I can stomach, meals are all too frequently greeted by me screwing up my face in disgust at the beautiful meal she has spent hours lovingly preparing for me. However, the woman is a legend and will swiftly make my favourite "sick dish" of toast spread with Bovril and slices of tomato (don't knock it till you have tried it!!)

I love you Mum and can never express my gratitude sufficiently for the tireless efforts you are putting into my care. I will no doubt keep you updated as to my progress however it is time to get some sleep, so I am able to fight another day! Thanks again for all your kind thoughts and prayers.

I've got Cancer where?

Chapter 10

Why no skull & crossbones on the box?

We are halfway through the first phase of my treatment and let me tell you, this stuff is no joke!! I continue to try act like an old school hard man as appearing vulnerable is still something I find deeply uncomfortable, so my Jason Statham impression is coming along swimmingly…

My bullshit bravado aside, a moment of truth – this stuff blows, the only time I felt worse is when I had Swine Flu but I believe if the Zombie apocalypse ever becomes a real thing, Swine flu will be where it all begins!

As usual I digress, this stuff is harsh, the effects of treatment are cumulative, so you feel worse as time goes on. You are permanently nauseous, your hands and feet are super sensitive, narcolepsy becomes a condition you finally understand but worst of all is "chemo brain", the simplest of tasks/conversations is nigh on impossible… sigh …

I am not having fun, however I know that the worse I feel means that the treatment continues to work so won't grumble (much…), I also recognise more and more that I am one of the lucky ones, every day I hear so many stories of people my age and younger who are diagnosed at Stage 4 so for whom the future is more terrifying, some of whom the cancer has spread to a point which is inoperable and they are facing palliative care rather than fighting for a win therefore am grateful I was diagnosed when I was and realise to feel a bit rubbish for a while is a small price to pay.

So, at this point I will soldier on and practice my British Bulldog impression in the mirror and when nobody is looking will sneak off to snivel quietly in the corner where the only audience is my loyal fuzz nugget, Dave! Thanks again for all the loving support

Chapter 11

The funnier side of chemo!

While there is little about chemo that is funny, there have been a few incidents because of "chemo brain" that have made me chuckle and not being one to take myself too seriously thought them worth a share.

Some of the things I have done which seemed perfectly normal to me at the time:

- Putting hand wash on my toothbrush; (not sure "lavender fresh" will ever catch on as a dental hygiene product catch phase)

- Straightening my hair for about 10 minutes before realising the bloody things were not on! Thought I was just having a particularly bad hair day.

- Trying to crush garlic with a can opener (yes, I did get as far as trying to put the clove in the thing and staring at it rather confused for an unacceptable period.

  Taking some other poor soul's trolley in Aldi and not realising until they politely pointed out my mistake after having made it to the next aisle already.

- Not realising I had doubled up on underwear until going in for treatment (I chose to ignore the confused stares of the radiotherapy team who were thankfully too polite to comment!)

In conjunction with the above I nearly overdosed my precious pup due to my inability to follow simple instructions on the medication package, I have now relinquished all complex and semi complex tasks to the family for fear of killing someone (ok, simple tasks too – better safe than sorry – there is the very real risk of caustic soda ending up in someone's tea!)

So, the next time you see someone staring at the button choices at a pedestrian crossing with a look of sheer panic in their eyes, be patient and kind, they could be stuck in a chemo haze and that one button could just be a decision too far for them to make unaided x

Chapter 12

The physical/mental warfare of Cancer treatment!

I apologise for the constant whinging, but I said I would be honest in my documentation of this phase and I plan to do just that. I also suspect my memory of this period will be a haze and maybe it seems a bit masochistic but I don't want to forget, If I am ever facing a challenge which seems overwhelming this blog is a reminder of how strong I can be when needed. I have never understood the stories where terminal cancer patients decide to stop treatment and opt for quality of life; I mean survival is our strongest instinct right?

If I were in their position and I got the choice 6 months of quality living over 2 years of being on treatment the choice would be simple, it would be a fantastic 6 months!! Before you all start gasping in horror, I am not terminal and there is the real chance of me being in remission within the next 9 months so there is no choice to make, I will grit my teeth and get through it. Let me walk you through a day in my life so you understand. Be warned, I hide nothing as this disease is not glamorous and the treatment is less so.

I wake up and within minutes I take Anti-sickness medication because if I don't you need to scrape me off the bathroom floor, your body continues to try get rid of the poison long after there is nothing left in your stomach. I have to take these tablets 3 times a day as the nausea NEVER goes away. Let's talk 'water works", holy cow!!! Having poison flowing through your system is only going to end one way, with a blazing Urinary Tract infection. For those who have never had one of these, every time you empty the old tank it is like you are peeing acid and razor blades, ladies many of you will know what I'm saying …

I have no immune system so my body cannot heal itself, so the misery is ongoing. I permanently feel like I have been kicked in the stomach by a horse, it hurts, ALL the time … pain is so debilitating when it is never-ending so knowing that within the next hour I need to take more of the "devil tablets" which are causing me to feel so horrendous is mental torture. I know they are saving my life, but I cannot bring myself to love them. My nerve endings in my hands are being damaged by the chemo, I have permanent pins and needles in my hand, I feel like I have ants crawling around inside my skin, creepy! This may or may not come right, fingers crossed as it is beyond weird.

The foodstuff I can tolerate, toast with Bovril, Steak pies, Pickled onions … nutritionally deficient? Yes! But it is ALL I can stomach, despite knowing my body needs nutritious food right now, I just can't do it. I cannot smell, see or even think of most food without my stomach turning. I watched MasterChef on TV the other night and there was a fish dish that literally made me heave. It is the strangest thing I have ever experienced.

A note to carers, dieticians and anybody responsible for the care of a cancer sufferer, don't take it personally when we reject your healthy culinary offering, we know it is good for us, but we just cannot face it. For Supermum whose world centres around health and nutrition this has been SO hard, but as she said it has been an education – on paper what we should be doing looks great, the reality however is very different! I am rapidly approaching the end of this phase and I am counting the hours; I will be one happy girl when I get to ring the bell as is the tradition at the end of treatment. There is still plenty to come but I get a bit of a break which is a welcome relief. Sorry this post is lacking any humour but for now all my energy is being used to just get through the day.

I've got Cancer where?

Chapter 13

Phase 1 over, I should be delighted, shouldn't I?

Today I got to ring the bell in the Radiotherapy unit signifying the end of treatment. A much-anticipated event in any Cancer sufferers' journey. The ringing of the bell is applauded by all in the unit as it is a symbol of hope for all undergoing treatment. So, you would expect this to be a happy occasion, wouldn't you? And yet I woke up this morning to a feeling of terror, the realisation that after today I am no longer having active treatment.

While there is more treatment to come, I now have a period of nothing, initially I anticipated this being a relief as my life can go back to normal for a while. There is no going back, that normal no longer exists. There is simply a lull during which I must wear a brave face and hope the cancer has responded to the treatment, that the tumour has shrunk enough to have the surgery to finally remove it. I need get past the fear that the cancer will make use of this time and grow and/or spread.

However, I think for now I need to feel this feeling and allow myself the time to get through it, denying it will be counterproductive. Hopefully I can find a sense of calm to get me through this time. Thank you again for all your love and support, it makes each step easier .

Chapter 14

Hurrah for the mundane!

I have come out the other side of the treatment and feel marvellous. I am back on my full protocol and living as healthy a life as possible, I recognise this is the time to build my body back up again for round 2 which I suspect will make round 1 feel like a gentle warm up before an ultra-marathon!

I got over my moment of terror quite quickly, predominantly because I lack the mental capacity to hang on to a feeling for too long, I find it energy sapping. Yup, no holding grudges for me, I will be mad at you for about a minute before … "Oh look! A squirrel".

So, with the cloud of doom having been whisked away I have gotten back to the usual drudgery of housework and life planning. Been bloody marvellous!

Steve and I have formulated a master plan to buy a caravan in the next 18 months. I did have to take a minute to look at myself and wonder at which point I became that person who gave up the life of parties and wild spontaneity and became a "caravan" person …

I believe it was around age 41 when any spontaneous action seemed to result in some form of physical discomfort and I resigned myself to the fact that careful consideration should be given to any future activities, this folks, is when you become "a caravan person"! I feel slightly ashamed and proud at the same time that I can tell you from just looking at a caravan on the motorway what the internal layout of said van is!

Much to the horror of my youngest son, Steve and I spend hours watching YouTube reviews on the latest models of caravan and if it has a tall fridge/ freezer and solar panelling oh my days, the oohs and aahs abound! It is official, we are sitting on the top of life's hill looking down the slope on the other side.

The point of making you sit through my waffle dear reader is because for now my world is not about cancer, I have been able to shelve the fear and have very quickly gone back to normal, I know it is there and I know there is more misery to come but for now my obsession is not about cancer, chemo, radiotherapy, haemoglobin levels, white blood cell or platelet counts, it is about the plush interior of the 2017 model Sterling Elite with the Smart controls that makes Steve grin like a Cheshire cat! My cup runneth over!

I head back to work next week and I am extremely excited, as I have pointed out my work colleagues are like family to me, the support they have given me during this dark time has moved me to tears. I am so looking forward to getting back and seeing them all but most of all to going back to feeling like I have a purpose.

My blogs are likely to be sparse for a while as while I am delighted at the prospect of going back to normal life it does not make for stimulating reading and I won't put you through it. In two weeks however, a group of us will be doing the Race for Life to raise funds for Cancer Research UK. I initially set a target of £500, I am very proud to say we have raised nearly £700. I will no doubt post some tales and photos of this great event and let you know if I managed to get my extremely sloth like self around the course.

I've got Cancer where?

Chapter 15

Team Blue in a sea of pink!

Well we did it, the gang and I participated in the local Race for Life to raise funds for Cancer research UK. An event which takes place across the UK at several different locations, always well attended. On Sunday the field was made up of 2,800 participants. The funds raised by this group alone was more than £270,000!!! This all goes to Cancer Research, with support like this it is a matter of time before this disease becomes a manageable condition rather than the killer it is today.

Traditionally the colour of choice for the Race for Life is pink, but as the colour of my Cancer is not pink Team Janine arrived kitted out in blue ready to earn all the pennies pledged.

You look around at all the faces in the crowd and you read the messages of support and it is deeply moving. Many participants have fought or are still fighting the disease or are friends/family that have had to watch loved ones suffer through treatment and many of those loved ones have lost their battle.

Despite all the emotions felt by the crowd the overriding feeling is one of unity, we all have a common goal and it is this that gets you across the finish line no matter how tired. So special!

Cancer itself brings little joy to the world, but I will tell you what its presence does do, it brings out the best in people and restores one's belief that mankind is inherently good. I could tell countless stories of people's kindness and generosity through this journey however it is the kindness of strangers that truly leaves me speechless, something that is truly rare for me as I can talk for all of England (and Wales, Scotland, Ireland, France etc, you get the gist!)

In preparation for the Race, Nades decided that to support the cause of raising awareness of Bowel Cancer she was going to brave the shave and die her hair blue (the colour of the bowel cancer ribbon). See below for the before and after. This woman is my dearest friend in the whole world and one of the kindest people I know. How many people do you that would be willing to undergo such a drastic transformation for a friend? Now obviously when I referred to the kindness of strangers it was not Nades I was referring to.

We were referred by some dear friends to Simply Hair in Melton Mowbray who would be the creative masterminds behind this transformation. We spent a good few hours with the wonderful Jason and Cerys from Simply Hair who treated me and Nades to our lovely new hairdos and then at the end of it all refused to take any payment. These were not long-time friends but people who we had only met hours before. Today at work one of my lovely colleagues told me that I was such an inspiration, I was so touched by this. Having given this, some thought I realised I am not the inspirational one, I have no choice but to follow the path I am on, however the people who have taken time out of their lives to support me, generously donated money to my fundraiser and been there to simply hold my hand through the tough times, it is all of you who deserve to be applauded as you gave when you didn't have to so I thank you profusely for everything.

A final note, I got my appointment letter for my CT scan which will be on the 3rd of August, we should find out soon after if the tumour has responded to the treatment so all going well I will be able to have the surgery which will kick off the next phase of my treatment so keep your fingers crossed.

I've got Cancer where?

Chapter 16

Here we go again!

After nearly three months of "normal" life we are back to the world of cancer. Thanks to the past few months being very busy at work I managed to take a mental break from the fears and stress this disease brings to your life and focus on a completely different stress, it's been great (she says through gritted teeth!) While I am sure you would all love to listen to me whine about the challenges of recruitment in the current market, I am going to disappoint you all and keep that exciting tale to myself!

So, where are we at? I had my CT and MRI scans a few weeks back to see how things were getting on. I discovered that the brains behind the terminology describing the tumours response to treatment must be the same people who feel the need to shatter the illusion of Santa and the Tooth Fairy!!! I was told that I had a "moderate" response to treatment... *MODERATE???*

This word to an over achiever is like a stake to the heart, it is like a lukewarm cup of tea, do you get where I am going with this? My competitive spirit was bruised, and I was not happy (it was not fear but the lack of a clear win that was really grating my carrot!)

However, when given a detailed explanation of what had gone on in there it was a moment in my head filled with applause and high fives!!

The tumour has reduced in size and the best news was the disease that was originally evident in the lymph nodes has dissolved. Take that you filthy little so and so!! What this means good people is I am now eligible for surgery. The method of butchery for me is an Anterior Resection, basically they cut out a section of my bowel and stick it back together.

Best case scenario procedure to be done laparoscopically, worst case they have to slice me open. Either way, not bothered because scars are cool, and it will make for great fun when my grandchildren arrive, I mean why would they not believe that Grandma fought off a gang of Pirates and all she got was a little cut??

The plumbing will be temporarily disconnected and I will be having an Ileostomy which is where they take a section of my small intestine and pull it out through my stomach to make a funnel thing through which I will … uuummm … pass waste. Hee, sorry – I can imagine all the "eeewww gross" comments. I got to bring a bag home today so I can torture my youngest with it … When waving it in his face all he could say was "gross Mom" … having kids is SSSOOO much fun! I laugh but must admit, this is the only part of my treatment which is leaving me a little apprehensive, the reason for this is I have visions of the bag exploding on me, and I have had the unfortunate experience of witnessing someone who has suffered this fate.

Before I started my treatment, I was having a particularly bad episode where I had to go into hospital and while in triage there was a gentleman whose bag had pretty much leaked everywhere, the poor chap looked absolutely mortified. While my heart went out to him all I could think was "that's going to be me!!!" But this is a case of short-term pain for long term gain, so just have to suck it up and get on with it.

Within 8 weeks of my surgery I will start the mop up chemo which from my previous experience I am sure is going to blow goats! But again, while I will no doubt grumble all the way through, I will get through it with an attempt at a smile.

I am hoping to be able to work through much of the next few months as I have realised that my job while at times can be "tear my hair out" frustrating, it is SO important to me, at the risk of sounding like a cliché, I love going home feeling like I have achieved something, somehow, I have added value, even if it is a small win it is enough to make me happy. If I can do this it can only make the next few months that little bit more bearable.

I will hopefully have my date for surgery within the next few days so will be able to plot out the next few months and fingers crossed squeeze in a few more weekends away in our beloved Vivienne before the fight begins. Vivienne for the confused among you is our caravan.

Chapter 17

It's a date!

On the 9th of October, almost 7 months to the day from diagnosis they will be going in and removing the uninvited guest that has taken up residence in my colon, hooray! Many ask if I am nervous, the answer is always no. I hate knowing that I have a part of my own body that is currently trying to kill me, I am carrying it around, feeding it and giving it everything it needs to thrive and grow. I just want it gone!

I went for my pre- assessment appointment last week, which was painfully long, 5 hours of meeting the various members of the team who will be looking after me on the day. As always, a great bunch of folks who filled me with confidence that I was in good hands.

One should never have favourites in your care team, particularly as one group of them will be armed with very sharp objects and may take being awarded 2nd place personally... gulp ... However, I must say, the Stoma Nurses are just awesome. It seems a characteristic requirement for this job is a wicked sense of humour and let me tell you, they all have it.

From the minute I walked into the office I was in hysterics, for women who literally deal with shit all day they rock! Our relationship soured a little when they said dried fruit is off the table … my mind instantly did a few sums and realised that Christmas is fast approaching and this takes mince pies off the table, a Christmas with no mince pies … just think about that for a second, did you get that sinking sensation in your stomach too?

I suppose I should explain the dried fruit thing, with an Ileostomy the stoma which is the exit point from your body is not that large and is prone to blockages, dried fruit tends to swell and can stop the works which will see me checked into one of the NHS's fine facilities for a period to clear it. Ugh, no mince pies for me.

The rules for ileostomy management are take small bites and chew your food properly, being a child, whose eating habits were formed at a boarding school where it is common practice to inhale your food for fear of missing out, this will be like learning to eat again. Supermum will be so happy as she is constantly reminding me to slow down. Watch this space to see if an old dog can learn new tricks. So, at this appointment I got marked up for where the stoma bag is to be placed. See below.

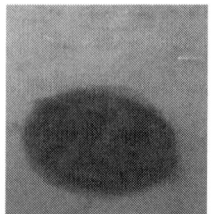

However, as my operation is a month away, I was sent away with my very own surgical pen to keep colouring in my dot... *big grin appears on face*... Meet Stan the Stoma Man!!! Let's hope my surgeon has a sense of humour...

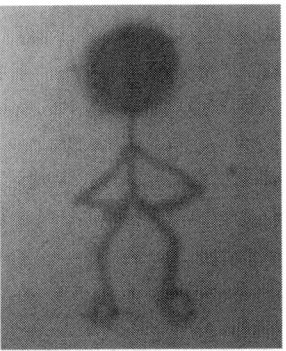

I've got Cancer where?

Chapter 18

Change of plan …

As they say, best laid plans and all that! I got a phone call from my surgeon's office on Friday to tell me they want to bring my operation date forward by a week. My new date is now the 1st October, this is a Sunday so still wondering if the lady got the date wrong and I will end up wondering the halls of Leicester General in my fetching hospital gown with my derrière hanging out looking for someone armed with a scalpel only to discover he is home enjoying a Sunday roast … suppose I will find out soon enough.

I am conflicted about this change, while they cannot get this monster out of me soon enough this means we have one week to get all our ducks in a row at work so my team are not left trying to pick up the pieces of my muddled thinking. This disease is a swine however as a result of its presence and my resulting absence from work, a wonderful lady stepped in to take my place and I can never thank her enough. An unflappable lady with many years of experience under her belt threw her hat in the ring and took on the challenge and has since proven to be an absolute superstar of the HR world. Stop sniggering you lot, HR is nothing, but rock n roll I tell ya, a life full of thrills and never-ending excitement… nod and smile folks, nod and smile!

To my team, sorry to abandon you again but I leave knowing that the department will be in safe hands. I had a moment the other day, to set the scene, I announced at a meeting that I had been given my operation date and before could continue to say why this news was relevant, one of my colleagues said, "Oh enough now, we are all bored already!" This was said totally in jest I hasten to add before you judge this person harshly. My reaction however was, "Aaaaaargh, is that really what people are thinking?"

However, this got the old grey matter going and I realised that I am constantly trying to pretend that life is normal and I try not to talk about my cancer as the last thing I want is people to be thinking "Oh my God woman, shut up already, you are so last year's news". Hence my reaction to an innocent joke. But there is a downside to this approach I have discovered, act like you are well and not terrified out of your wee little mind and people naturally accept this is the case. The expectation then is for you to be, do and deliver as you have before. So, in order not to appear weak and feeble you step up and do just that, all the while your body is screaming at you not to.

Why am I so afraid of appearing vulnerable? Why is the thought of failure, even under these extreme circumstances utterly terrifying? Why do I never feel good enough, smart enough or successful enough to the point where I will overdo it to a degree where I physically suffer as God forbid the world may think I am a flake if I don't? Surely in itself this behaviour is a weakness! To be able to show the world that you are sick and afraid is surely a sign of strength rather than the bullshit pretence to avoid pity. One to ponder methinks.

They say cancer is the biggest fight you will ever have, and I agree this may be true. But I think the bigger demon I need to contend with is the one in my head. I don't need to be everything to everyone all the time, it is ok not to be perfect, just to be enough for me. So, if all the reasons I had to beat this disease weren't already enough then here is one more to add to the pile, get better and sort my shit out!

I've got Cancer where?

Chapter 19

Sliced and diced!

I am sitting here trying to capture my experience of the past week while being divebombed by a bloody fly, needless to say I can't concentrate and my physical limitations are becoming very apparent as I cannot lift my arms above my head to take it out with a shoe (can't even lift the shoe!) but I did nearly stun the lil sucker by throwing a fully loaded box of ibuprofen at him.

Ok, I missed him by a mile as I move slower than a three-legged tortoise now, but had it been last week his ass would have been mine. Steve saved the day and the fly is no longer a problem.

So, our week started with my op being set for Sunday, I then get a phone call telling me it had been moved to Monday, I then received a letter saying op was on Monday but I still needed to go in on Sunday for a pre-op consultation. We get to the hospital at 7h30 Sunday morning to be told it was a mistake and they in fact did not need to see me until the Monday.... sigh ...

But Monday morning comes around and I have scrubbed myself from head to toe with the antibacterial soap and am bloody starving so hope we can get this show on the road pronto, we arrive at the hospital and were told I was first on the list, excellent! And then, someone more in need than me had to get into theatre first so I was bumped into second place so only went in at about 1pm. But they took pity on me and gave me a cup of water … thanks a bunch… this would be where I would place the snarky faced emoji!!

Was wheeled down to theatre to have at least my third conversation of the day which goes like this "where is that accent from?" "Oh, where in South Africa are you from?" (I just answer Durban, it cuts out at least a third of this conversation) and the final, "why did you move to Leicester?". Yup, gotta love the small talk that avoids having to address the elephant in the room, "so, you have cancer? That sucks man!"

Got to theatre where a bright shiny eyed little chap stated that he was doing medicine, and would I object to him observing? "Knock yourself out kid, if seeing me in my paper knickers hasn't made you lose your lunch the rest should be a breeze" So, they gave me the anaesthetic which sent me off to lala land and the next thing I recall was waking up in the ward feeling like someone had taken a chainsaw to my stomach … I cannot funny this one up, it was brutal and unfortunately at the point I woke up my sweet son came in to see me with tubes sticking out of everywhere and moaning more than just a little about the pain. My poor child didn't take it well.

The procedure I had was called a Lower Anterior Resection, this was all done laparoscopically with the surgeon driving little robot arms, I decided to watch a YouTube video of the procedure being performed and then I realised why it is so painful, there is a lot of grabbing, pulling, burning going on and it aint pretty! But for those who like this kind of thing worth a watch, very impressive, don't know how they can tell what to cut, it all looks the same to me, slimy, icky and lots of it!

As I explained in previous posts I was told prior to going in that there was a 90% chance that I would be sporting an Ileostomy bag, a thing I dreaded however woke up to be given the news that this hadn't been necessary and I was stuck back together to function as normal. Would have done a happy dance but thought I would save it as would've ended in tears.

Have you ever noticed when you have a procedure done something will be casually mentioned such as in my case "after bowel surgery your bowel may not function for up to 24 hours after your surgery" and then they will move onto what to pack for your visit? This is like in exams of past, it may not seem like an important part of the question but is in fact THE most important part of the question. The first day of my recovery was spent counting the hours until the trolley carrying the morphine came my way again.

Oh, and pacing up and down the 100-yard corridor (I know it was 100 yards as it had floor markers measuring every 20 yards… who still measures in yards?) Back to corridor patrol; having read all the literature on accelerating one's recovery I knew that I had to suck it up and get on my feet ASAP as the longer I was on my ass, the longer I was going to hurt. This corridor was going to become my favourite stomping ground as it became obvious that the 24 hours anticipated for the bowel to start working was generous, try 72 hours.

Now I hear you ask why this is a big deal so I will tell you, the old poo pipe has had a decent size piece removed and has been stitched back together (already ouchie!) You are encouraged to eat straight away and so I religiously did so so 3 times a day, this all piles up putting enormous pressure on an area which is already feeling rather sore (being polite, it was f……..g agony!) I cannot describe what these 3 days felt like, but they will go down as some of my least favourite of all time. But I kept walking and we finally had a breakthrough. Terribly undignified I know but I ran (ok, hobbled) into the Nurses station proudly announcing to all around that the eagle had landed and all was well, they were all lovely enough to send me off with a round of applause while I went to share the news with my girls from ward 4 who too had been cheering me on whilst awaiting this momentous occasion.

So, on sharing this news with my consultant again the news delivered whilst applauding myself he very happily announced I was ok to be discharged and to keep up the good work. Yes, I was wearing the face of the proud toddler who had just been given her first pair of big girl knickers. So, I am pleased to say I am back home with a drain still attached as I am still leaking profusely from the op site but they said I seemed sensible enough to monitor the output and manage the whole thing myself for a few days …

I think truth be told they decided to have a woman with crazy hair prancing around the ward telling everyone who would listen that she had gone potty all on her own was proving to be a PR nightmare and to get the crazy bitch outta there! I am still bloody sore and expect to be for a while, but all in all it was a success and I am pleased with the outcome, even my scars are super cool!

Thanks for all the love and support y'all xx

Chapter 20

Histology report in, total win!

Hobbling around the supermarket today in the hunt for vegetables my phone rang, our local Tesco is a mobile signal dead zone so would normally ignore the call until I re-entered civilization. However, the caller showed as "private number", these calls are always from my consultant's office so I decided to head out and temporarily abandon my shopping and darling Nades who is up to visit for a few days to take care of the invalid.

I can now openly admit I have been absolutely terrified of getting the results back from my op, this is when they can truly tell you what's what and give you an accurate staging after treatment.

The news was the best I could have hoped for. The cancer was present in the original tumour however of the 14 lymph nodes removed there was no cancer found in any of them. The sense of relief is unbelievable, lots of hugs and tears in the veggie aisle, Nades even did a little jig, LOVE her to bits.

We will still be doing chemo as although there is little chance of rogue cells, we are going with the better safe than sorry approach. Not a long one tonight as I have got a Great British Bake off to watch but wanted to share this news. Today is a good day and for the first time in 7 months I am happy to look to the future.

Chapter 21

What evil deed earned me this punishment?

I have been feeling all smug of late due to the constant praise from folks regarding my rapid recovery from surgery, I have grown rather fond of the title of Superwoman … And then I met my new Oncologist today, Dr I. Don't get me wrong, I have already decided that this Nigerian Princess of medicine is just what I need to hold my hand through the next 6 months but for the first time in this journey the plan she has for me has filled me with dread. I was convinced that the chemo I would be getting was going to be harsh but manageable, it turns out that I am looking at 6 months of pure misery.

I will be having an infusion of Oxaliplatin (look it up, nasty stuff – many don't manage the full course due to nerve damage) followed by 2 weeks of Capecitabine, this the same chemo I had before, yup those tablets I was bleating about some months back, bloody awful stuff. I asked Dr I if the dosage would be reduced only to be disappointed with the answer.

The same dosage… ugh … I will have a break of a week and then the hell starts all over again. This is repeated 8 times over the next 6 months. This is where I am going to make a polite request to anyone who I am likely to see over the next few weeks, please don't say any of the below:

- **You can do it; you are so strong!** It is not about being weak or strong, I simply have no choice.

- **Just remember, it is saving your life.** As much as you think this knowledge would make you skip into the chemo ward singing "oh happy days", trust me … you don't, it is more "March of the damned" by Judas Priest.

- **Keep smiling, it will be over before you know it!** No, it won't, things that are over before you know it are luxury holidays, Christmas and one's youth, 6 months of chemo feels like an eternity!

I apologise if I sound grumpy and miserable, but I am going to allow myself this moment, the truth is I am tired, scared and lacking the energy I so desperately need to do this. So, if you do see me, just say one of the following:

- Would you like a cup of tea? Richard Hooper, colleague, friend and wind-up merchant – this one you nailed.

- I can't make it better, but I am here for you if you need me.

- And most importantly, "if you need to vent, I will quietly sit and listen" (this best combined with point 1)

Chapter 22

Capox round 1, Lord have mercy!

Here we are, round one done, I suspect I wouldn't feel so bad if I hadn't woken up with a cold yesterday. As I didn't have a temperature, we were ok to proceed. The Oxaliplatin infusion went well, your arm does hurt but it is manageable. I believe things get more interesting on round two. Always helpful being sat next to someone who has done this course of poison and declared it "the worst ever!" "Cheers mate, remind me to buy you a beer when this is all over as a show of thanks!!!" Sometimes honesty is not necessarily the best policy, I will take the version with the rose-tinted specs ta very much!

Anyway, back to now. Part of the treatment is a course of steroids, I have a suspicion my cold germs were lying in wait and did a snatch and grab on these bad boys and I now have a cold with serious guns and hectic "roid rage". My eyes have virtually disappeared into my face and my nose is prematurely getting into the festive spirit, could easily send Rudolph packing if I wanted a career change, I have never looked so pretty?!

Now this chemo is weird with a capital WHA! If I touch anything cold with my hands or feet it feels all prickly, like touching broken glass. If you drink anything below lukewarm your throat closes and feels awful, plus your tongue suddenly becomes very lazy and trying to say a word with an 's' in it is hilarious, superstitious is particularly entertaining for the listener. It does pass quite quickly so all good.

There is one side effect which I quite like, if you go out in the cold your face and lips kind of tingle, it is like having tiny snowflakes kiss your face, in my head it is how you would feel if you were sparkly, my youngest believes that is the steroids talking, he just doesn't get that the cold nicked all of them and left none for me and that I am transforming into Tinkerbell, ok, more of a plus sized, grey haired , ungainly version … so from now on I will be known as "Chunkerbell" Best I take my germ ridden sparkly self to bed. Will keep you all updated.

Chapter 23

Hot and bothered

Well, not really bothered so much but "hot & happy" would suggest this story belongs on a different kind of website; one with an age restriction! As predicted my treatment has brought on "the change"; that time in our lives most women dread as it brings with it the following:

- Weight gain, coupled with weight distribution to areas previously considered the more attractive parts of one's body, I mean seriously?? This is problematic as one no longer knows how to dress this unfamiliar physique, resulting in extensive wardrobe culls and failed shopping excursions, these being a failure largely due to high street retailers insisting on fitting out their dressing rooms with recycled items from a redundant House of Mirrors attraction.

  I know this is what they do as my derriere is NOT that wide or lumpy and I certainly don't have back fat. I know I still look like a Victoria's Secret model really (actually, did I ever....?)

- Increased financial burdens, purely due to the process of spending thousands on trying to put together a wardrobe that makes sense.

- Mood swings, although I suspect this is less to do with hormones and more the obvious outcome of points 1 & 2.

- Hot flushes …So, point 4 … imagine having your internal heating system go from comfortable room temperature to "standing in the Saharan desert in mid-summer at 12 noon", this is instant, no warning. I had one of these delightful episodes today. I sat down at my desk and within seconds had sweat pouring from every pore of my body, of course the natural thing to do is start frantically fanning yourself with the nearest suitable object to try taming the raging furnace within, however the increased physical activity did not help matters. Let's talk hair, I have battled with frizz for years, a hint of moisture in the air and "poof", I look like a distant relative of Albert Einstein.

So, in my opinion ladies and gents, "hot mess" describes a menopausal woman and does not actually mean "A person who is dishevelled who yet remains alluring" as is suggested by **http://www.urbandictionary.com**!

Now here is where my current predicament gets interesting, my body constantly feels about 100°c hotter than is humanly comfortable but the Oxaliplatin aka Poxy Oxy by us chemo kids causes cold sensitivity in ones extremities, hands, feet and tip of your nose, so when one of these hot flushes happens you are naturally tempted to run outside into the UK winter to cool off however when you do you develop an extreme case of pins and needles in the aforementioned body parts, and pins and needles in your nose aint no joke as this brings on a serious sneezing fit.

One blessing though is now the wardrobe issue is solved for the moment as until this is over, I am wearing nothing but summer clothes with thermal socks and mittens and one of those foam clown noses so I am ready at all times.

I have taken the liberty of including a self-portrait below, this may explain why I choose the written word as my creative medium rather than drawing or painting, those talents were awarded to my brother, along with the "I will always be thin no matter what I eat" and beautiful olive skin genes ... cheers Mum!

PS Still love your bro, even if you nicked all the good stuff out of the genetic cookie jar before I could get at it x

Chapter 24

Round 2 … What hit me?

Holy cow, I feel like I have been run over by a freight train… My whole body is hurting, the bone pain is unlike anything I've experienced to date. If I sneeze, I experience a severe stabbing pain in my eyes which frikkin kills, man alive this stuff is evil! The side effects have certainly ramped up this time and I am feeling pretty darn sorry for myself. But I know within a week or so I will be back to normal again, well … my definition of normal.

This week my chemo buddy was the super awesome Nades, she drove up to spend the day with me and sat with me while I had my infusion, naturally within 5 minutes of entering the chemo suite she had stolen the hearts of everybody there. As always, she kept me laughing and this is much needed as the infusion is pretty painful.

The chemo suite has a surprisingly upbeat atmosphere, considering what we are all doing there it is quite remarkable how chatty and cheerful everybody is. All my chemo neighbours this week were stage 4s, technically incurable. But not a glum face to be seen, we all had a good natter with a good few laugh. While nobody ever wants cancer, there is a part of me that is truly grateful to have been able to witness the strength of humanity in this environment.

I apologise if I am lacking my usual humour today, pain tends to rob me of my funny. I just wanted to let you know I am still breathing, and all is well. I must say thank you to all my devoted tea makers at work, you guys rock and those cups of tea are the best medicine.

Chapter 25

Why so low?

This past week has been a tough one, I don't know why it stands out from the rest, but it does. Maybe because I am currently living in this moment and feeling these emotions now, and the next time they come it will feel like I am at my lowest point again but the level is just in fact a repeat of the same I am experiencing today.

I feel pressure, pressure from work, from home, treatment, just everywhere and despite my support group doing everything to protect me from that pressure it is still there. I had a plan; I was going to power through treatment not allowing it to rob me of another moment of my life.

This round hurt me and showed me who was boss. I have kept trying to push back only to land flat on my ass again. This left a pile of anxiety filled self-pity that physically resembled me. I had to miss an important meeting at work because I was struck down by a chest infection, I felt sick, exhausted and to compound it a complete failure as a whole process ground to a halt because I couldn't get my sorry ass out of bed.

There are people at work who need my help and I lie huddled in my protective fluffy blanket cocoon contemplating my misfortune pretending the outside world does not exist. I watch my family rally around me catering to my every need while I simply sit and watch them do so, I fear Supermum will suffer burnout due to having to look after a 43-year-old toddler.

What is this about? Why do I suddenly feel paralysed? I can't seem to 'deal', and 'deal' is what I do, I love to take charge and make things happen. Everything just feels too much, and I don't know where to start! For the first time today I felt panic, I panicked about a recurrence and having to face this all again, I panicked that it had all just caught up with me and I was slowly starting to break. I panicked about losing me and never finding me again.

I wish I could tell you I go to sleep tonight having had an epiphany and that I knew the answer to my current dilemma, but I don't. I have tried counting my blessings of which I have so many, but this has not yet proven fruitful. Perhaps the answer is simply to put one foot in front of the other, and make lists, I like lists, I find the sense of order comforting. Yes, I will try this approach so hopefully my next blog may see the return of some humour as laughter is much needed in all our lives, I know it is certainly needed in mine.

Chapter 26

Round 3 – no whinging I promise

Woohoo, round 3 done! Was it horrid? Yes! Did it hurt? Yes! Do I feel like crap? Yes! Am I going to whinge? HELL NO! Not this time. I now have the advantage of prior knowledge and experience; I know what this stuff does and how it makes me feel and how long I am going to feel like poo. This makes it easier; you know when it ends and how long you gotta be a brave lil soldier. So, for now the pity party is over.

We have had a wonderful festive season, special time spent with family and friends. I got a chest infection so was isolated from society for a week which meant I missed the annual works Christmas do, but as always, the Marketing team made sure I was not left out and made a video for me of greetings from my much-loved colleagues. Lots of laughs and as many happy tears from yours truly, the love I have received and continue to receive from all of you is superfood for my soul.

Christmas Day was hosted by my ex Duncan Aka Grumpy and his beautiful better half Monika. What a spread Monika put on; the table was groaning under the weight of the most amazing Christmas meal I have ever had. My newly crafted bowel was frantically waving a white flag halfway through dessert. Thanks guys love you lots, although think my intestines are a little scared of you now!

Cancer has a way of changing one's life plans. As I have mentioned in my precious post S and I bought our house two years ago with the intention of renovating it, we were going to turn it into our dream home. Three weeks ago, I said to S "I am tempted to just find a readymade house", so here we three weeks later. We have sold our house and signed for our perfect readymade home. Impulsive much?

The reason for this sudden change of plans, I don't want to spend the next five to ten years pouring over paint swatches, seriously, all greys look the same to me anyway. I want to live life. I want to head off in Vivienne and enjoy this beautiful country and other distant shores. I want to spend time with friends and family. I want to get back on Miss Daisy (my super girlie lilac shopper bike) and cycle around the beautiful Leicestershire countryside.

So, end of February we move to a new house, problem is I have chemo on the 27th which renders me useless, ooops! Ssssooo, any of our friends based nearby, the offer of any help needed may now be called upon. We don't have exact dates yet but if you are free and willing Steve will probably be grateful for any extra hands. I hope you have all had a wonderful festive season filled with nothing but joy and love which will overflow into 2018 to start the New Year on a positive note. To all my Cancer buddies, may this year bring you good health and give you the ultimate gift of hearing those three words, "you're in remission"

I've got Cancer where?

Chapter 27

Goodbye 2017!

I so wish as we wave goodbye to 2017 that I was waving goodbye to my cancer story. I would love to be making a list of New Year's resolutions that there wasn't a cat in hells chance I would stick to for more than 5 days, you know, like the following:

- Lose three stone and get back to being as fit as I was in my early 20's. I could do this if jaw could be wired for six months and had several joints replaced. Listening to me walk up and down stairs is a symphony of clicks and grinding noises that I am fairly sure shouldn't be made by the human body.

- Become super organised Mum/career woman, for those of you who watch Madam Secretary, Tia Leoni's character is who I aspire to be, perfect parent while successfully governing the world's greatest superpower and always appearing flawlessly groomed. This one is tricky, to start I need to master the art of waking up before 8am and realising that the best the world is going to get from me today is clean and semi-conscious.

- Have a super organised home with that is always show room standard and guest ready. May need to enlist the skills of Supermum for this, this is definitely her bag, mine is more the "shift the crap around the house to be hidden in the 'bits and pieces drawer' to hide from guests when required".

But alas I cannot yet turn my back on the burden 2017 chose to hand to me just yet, I must continue to fight the fight until April so will have to shelve my plans to revolutionise myself until then and be content with the notion that the new house and new healthy (ish) body may prove a strong enough motivator for positive life change once I am physically and mentally capable.

As I reflect on this past year it has been hard, in my list of most difficult life challenges this is second only to the death of my late husband. My body feels like I have done 10 rounds with Mike Tyson. It will take me a long time to recover from the physical and psychological damage this disease has done to me. But I will.

However, this year has brought with it some of the greatest gifts I will ever receive, the realisation that I am loved, I have received a depth of love and support from family, friends and colleagues that have made me realise that I am worthy.

Despite not seeing myself as perfect, the people surrounding me see me as a good enough version of me to love me no holds barred. This tells me that should I never achieve the aforementioned goals that this won't make anybody love me anymore or any less. This is your gift to me, acceptance of self, who I am is perfect enough for you so thank you. My wish for all of you for 2018 is a year overflowing with prosperity, joy and love.

May your troubles be few and your successes plentiful.

I've got Cancer where?

Chapter 28

How wrong was I?

My plan was to work on the premise that I now know the devil so can look him square in the eye and tell him to "bring it on dude!" But the devil is a deceitful bastard, apparently anyway, not met him myself so I could be being completely unjust, he could just be misunderstood with tragic childhood issues …? But for now, we will just go on the character profile provided in all folklore and say he is a total shit!

Anyway, back to the point, the devil is a sneaky conniving con artist, lulling you into a false sense of security and then taking his pitchfork to the back of your head when you are not looking. The devil in my story is chemo! This round of chemo has chewed me up and spat me out, then stood on me and squished me into the floor, and then peed on me for good measure. I have for the first time through this whole drama sat and cried like a baby, and I am no crier, unless of course it is anything to do with my children or a dog dies in a movie then I am downright inconsolable!

My most frequent thought over the past week has been to take my chances with cancer as this is truly a living hell. Just a quick tutorial, for the eternal optimists out there, a word of advice. Do not offer up platitudes to someone in my position such as "what you are feeling is the drugs working so think of it as a good thing so keep it up", I can promise you that I will actually bite you, and I can assure you the toxicity of a bite from me right now would make that from a Komodo dragon feel like a mosquito bite!

So, as you have gathered the "no whinging" was not an option, each round does not just get marginally worse, it goes from a firm smack around the head with an open hand to "lets crack you full tilt around your noggin with a sledgehammer"

I am not looking for sympathy, I simply need to vent. The effect on my body has been utterly devastating but the knock-on effect that it has had on my mind is worse. I am scared of everyday things as I know they will hurt, my hands and feet getting cold is agony, so I refuse to go outside or touch anything cold. I am too scared to drink anything that is not hot as the sensation of my throat closing is awful to say the least. I am scared of drinking water, not just "I don't feel like it", I actually get extremely anxious taking a sip of anything.

Sound ridiculous? It does to me too. I wonder if studies have been done on chemo patients to establish whether many suffer from PTSD after the fact, I think the findings could be interesting. Again, I am not looking for sympathy, just a willing ear. I need to rage about this thing to keep what little sanity I have left intact.

Chapter 29

Feeling the fear

I had my follow up appointment with my surgeon last week to discuss my operation and ongoing treatment. I left that appointment feeling less than positive as some of the points he raised had the alarm bells in my head ringing at a deafening volume. He described the tumour as aggressive and stated that despite being told initially that I had a reasonable response to the chemoradiotherapy, when he cut me open the tumour had hardly shrunk at all meaning I had in fact had a poor response. I wonder if cancer takes on the personality of its host, if so, I am deep in the "do-do"!

The shrieking voices in my head interpreted this as meaning that I generally don't respond well to chemo, so does this mean that the hell I currently find myself in will do little more than batter my body but any rogue cancer cells will laugh in the face of the chemo?

I have an image of a playground fight between a bunch of hard-core, tattooed skinhead cells donning leather jackets and the hall monitor equivalent, you know, the ones empowered on paper but in reality, they are still going to get their asses handed to them when they hit the real world.

Let's just hope that the Oxaliplatin is the Bruce Lee of chemo's and takes out the schoolyard bullies through a stealth attack when they are not looking! The other thing he said to me was that it is a bad thing to get cancer when you are young as there is a higher chance of a recurrence.

I would assume this is the case as in reality at 42 you have a lot more years left on this planet therefore logically if you have a predisposition there is a lot more opportunity for it to return. It seems however the reason is more biological; this is the point where I curse myself for spending my time in Science messing about with the Bunsen burners and not actually listening to the teacher.

Supermum says it is to do with your metabolic system being faster. If this is the case, I am super grateful for having no thyroid and the metabolism of a sloth, I may never be supermodel skinny but I will take that over this disease popping up again for a repeat visit.

So, I went away from that appointment feeling rather bummed out and did the worst thing possible, went onto Google. The stats suggest that as a stage 3 there is a 50% chance of a recurrence, not awesome odds (unless given against a lottery win), this news left me feeling somewhat morbid, however after a good night's sleep I gave myself a mental slap and was fine again.

What will be will be and worrying about it won't make any difference to the outcome. I am afraid, I still find it hard to plan too far into the future, but I am sure over time this will get easier. I go in for round 4 this Wednesday, I am of course dreading it as each time it gets harder and the side effects more horrific. But on the upside this treatment is the halfway mark so that is something to celebrate, will raise a shot of Gaviscon to the universe to mark the occasion.

I've got Cancer where?

Chapter 30

Ouch!

Well, we are back in the misery which is post infusion, but you have heard about that over and over so should you wish for a refresher please refer to previous posts.

I went in for my infusion on Wednesday, usual routine. Check in, go through to the day room where all us patients compare side effects and generally have a bit of a giggle at some of the ridiculous things our bodies are doing. The weird face paralysis thing being one of them as is evident in the photo at the end of this chapter, couldn't manage a smile as left side of face kept going into a spasm.

The same keeps happening to my hands, it aint a good look. Fingers crossed it is not permanent (best not cross fingers as they may bloody stay that way forever!) You then get called through to get hooked up to your pump and personal cocktail mix. Have tried to order a Cosmo or Margarita mix but to date no joy … humph!

So, this Wednesday my usual nurse the gorgeous and wonderful Faye was not assigned to me, instead I had a new nurse. As soon as she started getting set up, I realised she was no seasoned veteran, the anxiety that was obvious on her face was extremely telling … this did not bode well. She struggled to find a vein and it felt like she was digging at my hand with an ice pick. When she finally got the cannula in, she looked at me and said, "that went well, I have really struggled with cannulating my patients today and yours is the best so far!".

Say what now? I had visions of patients with great big holes in their hands being wheeled across to A&E to be patched up before being returned to endure the trauma all over again.

Apparently, this poor young lady has only been doing this for a week, I really felt for her as it must be so difficult as your patients are already in pain and grumpy when being attacked with needles in veins that are already battle scarred and not terribly forgiving. Needless to say, my hand smarted the whole way through the infusion and is now developing a beautiful bruise. But no grudges here, we all have to start somewhere, and I can only hope I get my lovely Faye back next time, the girl operates a cannula like a fairy does a wand.

The news has been filled with reports on the Aussie Flu epidemic, this has made ours a slightly nervous household. With my immune system being as effective as a fart in a thunderstorm we have become hyper vigilant about screening of visitors. Please don't be offended if we quiz you on recent exposure to sickness before letting you into the house, I feel terribly rude doing this but the NHS is already short on beds so doesn't need to add lil ol' me to the list.

My darling mother-in-law has even been scouring the shops and hunting online for an antibacterial gel that has more than 62% alcohol content (required level to kill off bugs I have recently learnt). We now have an industrial size bottle which sits at the door for visitors to liberally use before entering the isolation unit that our home has become. Just love that woman.

Otherwise life is much the same, I feel like crap and my poor family continues to suffer as they cater to my every whim without even so much as a mumble. Saints alive do I ever owe them when this is done?! But it has been a good week overall, got the mortgage offer so all systems go for our new home which we move into at the end of February. That is the 'Royal we' of course, I am likely to be sitting at my mum-in-laws all snug under my favourite blankie accompanied by our precious fuzz nugget Dave while Steve and a few helpers do all the work. Seriously guilt ridden about this but unfortunately not much I can do. But will attempt to make up for it as best I can.

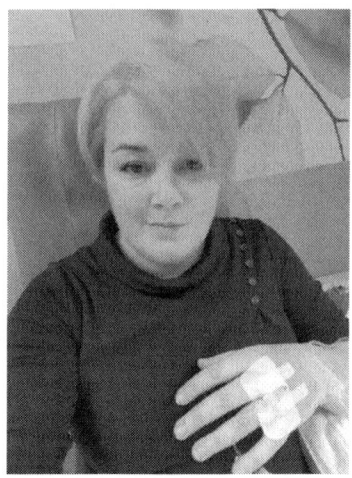

Chapter 31

I want …

I want to hide from this, I no longer want to be brave. I want to wake up and not feel sick and in pain. I want to be back in a place where I am no longer shrouded in a depressive fog. I want to stop being jealous of everyone around me doing normal every day. I want my life back. I hate this! This is a cycle of misery that seems to have no end, the brief reprieve of the one or two days before your next cycle begins where you feel you are almost human again only serves as torture as you know that soon it will be stolen away in the blink of an eye.

I know I go on and on about this hell, and I so wish I had something new to say, but this hell is all I am about right now. I am sorry I keep repeating myself, but I need to voice my pain for my own sanity. The cold is my enemy, I fear it more than anything. The side effect is named "cold sensitivity", but it robs you of the ability to do the simplest of tasks. Things I can no longer simply just do:

- I cannot open a door or drawer; the handle is too cold.

- I cannot take anything from the fridge or freezer, it is too cold.

- I cannot prepare food for meals; it is too cold.

- I cannot touch the keyboard of my laptop to remain connected with the world, it is too cold.

- I cannot touch taps; they are too cold.

- I cannot pick up a cup, plate or knife and fork without someone warming them up for me, they are too cold.

- I cannot go outside; it is too cold.

I do any of the above without thinking and the result is agony, every nerve feels like it is on fire, like being electrocuted. All I do every day is sit and stare into space, I can do nothing as I am helpless, I am like a child again and I hate it. I shed no more tears of self-pity; I am simply numb. I understand why so few people complete this regime. It is torture, nothing less.

Chapter 32

Feeling the love

Well, it is 3:45am and I have concluded that tonight's experiment of trying to get to sleep without the aid of my trusty sleeping tablets has proven a complete failure... oh well! I thought perhaps I could use this time to put together a post that wasn't all "snot en trane" (for my non-Afrikaans speaking audience the direct translation is snot and tears, it just sounds better in Afrikaans!)

My side effects sadly continue to plague me, but I have come out of the "dark place" as I have come to call it. I know I go on about the kindness and generosity shown to me, but it still makes my heart swell every time somebody does something to show they care. I have often mentioned the tireless efforts of Supermum, Steve and my super special Nades, but I just feel I want to share the following as I want you lot to know how much it meant to me.

- Last week one of my work buddies popped in to visit and gave me the most beautiful orchid, every time I see it I don't see a flower, I see that I am loved, Dickie, you have been a true mate, love ya!

- After my post about the cold hands and feet Steve arrived home with a gift from another work mate, warm socks and self-heating hand gel packs … like frikkin AMAZING things! Diane, you rock!

- Last week when I was feeling particularly low, an envelope dropped through the door, it was a beautiful card with a heart-warming message from an ex work colleague Emma whom I adore beyond words, (and she is a fellow Saffa so gets extra brownie points)

- Last Friday before having to rush off to Poland to deal with a family emergency, our beautiful Kasia (our Polish Princess) came over to make me a batch of chicken soup that I love. You know I love you and Cecil beyond words and as I said to you last week, so glad we won custody of you in the divorce!

- Someone else who constantly shows how much she cares through gifts of lovely delicacies and supportive messages is my ex-husbands beautiful partner, Monika. This wonderful lady not only joined our crazy crew and accepted the "weird" dynamic of our family but has been one of my most constant cheerleaders.

- Finally, Steve arrived home with another gift from another friend from work, also called Emma, again after the "cold hands" complaint this precious package contained USB heated gloves!!! I know right? Like totes amazeballs!!! The young lady from whom the gift came is currently going through a particularly challenging time herself. On opening the card and seeing who it was from I promptly dissolved into a messy pile of tears (and I said I wasn't a crier!!) The fact that despite everything going on in her world she still thought of me moved me more than you will ever know.

So, the point of all of this is, I will struggle, I will get sad, I will want to give up. But it is the little things that you all do that keep me going. You will never know how far your constant show of love and support is carrying me through this difficult period. Thank you, thank you, thank you xxx

Chapter 33

Round 5 done, hurrah!

Well, we are more than halfway there, three sessions left – hurrah! On Monday met with my Oncologist the ever-glamorous Dr I. We decided that it was time to reduce the Oxaliplatin dosage as the side effects were continuing past the 10-day deadline i.e. they never went away … gggrrr!

Dr I was confident that as I have had 50% of my chemo which is the mainstay of my treatment regime it would have no impact on the efficacy of the protocol. Also discussed was the "dark place", I reasoned that as it happens without fail by day 4 and then passes there must be a reason for it. Apparently, this is caused by coming off the steroids, also known as a steroid crash, the symptoms being severe depression, anxiety, mood swings. Happy dance!! Not losing me marbles!!

So today I was given 75% of my original dose. I left the chemo suite full of optimism that this must mean the immediate side effects of the infusion would be minimal, so I did the neuropathy test which is touch various cold/metal objects to gauge sensitivity, railing outside the hospital being first choice … discovered new found optimism unfounded, some yelping and strange looks from passers-by left me feeling a little stupid. My face then joined the party and started doing the "Elvis" and as I had forgotten my snood I had to cover my face with my hands which is slightly awkward in a lift, I felt the need to explain myself to the other occupants of the lift as didn't want them to think I was suggesting that they smelled bad, the thought probably would not even have occurred to them but thought it was best to be sure.

It is always good to see my chemo day gang; I am always genuinely happy to see them and know that they have come through their last session relatively unscathed. While I look forward to the end of this nightmare, I will miss them. As many of them are terminal cases I know their story will not have a happy ending, and selfishly am glad I will never know when their story ends as these wonderful souls have in their own way made this easier for me and the thought of them not being around for the rest of the world to meet and come to love is too sad to consider.

Unfortunately, one of our regulars had a nasty reaction to her chemo today which was hard to witness, she always attends on her own so my heart went out to her as having such a violent reaction is difficult enough without having a loved one there to hold your hand. Sending lots of love and positive thoughts to her via the universe tonight.

Chapter 34

Familiarity breeds contempt?
Perhaps not ....

So, we are back in that dark place filled with pain and misery, what is interesting this time is I simply accept it for what it is. There is no fighting it, I just need to ride the storm. This does not make it any more pleasant mind, but acceptance has brought slight relief.

Somehow the halfway mark of the treatment held no relief but having only three cycles of treatment left for some reason does, perhaps it is simple maths, the majority is behind me and the side effects are no longer getting worse and while they remain at "bloody horrendous" they are no worse than last time, this is a win, nothing new or unknown to contend with is always a bonus.

Although the cold sensitivity in the hands does still on occasion cause a temper tantrum that would be the envy of any hot-blooded diva, we are talking the hurling of objects against walls coupled with language that would make your hair stand on end. Not very dignified but I have managed to refrain from the launching of anything expensive or that shatters so at least the damage is minimal.

As mentioned, we are moving to a new house in two weeks, what makes for interesting timing is the same day we move is the date of my next chemo infusion … oops!

So, while I sit in my recliner being topped up on poison while being served tea and dodgy sandwiches; Steve, his wonderful family and his boss Phil who is taking the day off to help will be moving home for me. Yes, I continue to harp on about it but want to make sure I record all the wonderful acts of generosity people have shown me. There will be moments in my life where I get frustrated with humanity and this blog will serve as a reminder that people are inherently good and kind as I have seen it in abundance over the past year (my battle started exactly 11 months ago today). I never want to forget nor take for granted the people who have given so much of themselves to help me, nor do I want to miss an opportunity to pay it forward wherever, whenever and for whomever I can.

I know my blog started out as funny but over time has become more serious, this is mildly concerning as I have spent most of the past 43 years managing to avoid "adulting" as it just didn't look fun. The question is do I embrace the change or go do some stupid stuff to reset the balance? Not sure I am a super fan of Serious Sally; the girl needs some lightening up. Any suggestions as to activities that could reset the balance? Nothing that involves nudity mind, it is too cold here and will make people cry …

Chapter 35

The end of the IV line

Well, it seems despite the reduction of the dosage of the "poxy oxy", the cumulative effects of the hell drug are literally too much for my nerves too handle. My hands and feet are now numb which feels a bit like trying to walk on somebody else's feet, just weird!

So, as with so many before me they need to stop the infusions. I would love to act the brave little soldier and tell you that I am disappointed and so wish I could stay the course but that would be a lie, I am dancing a jig of pure joy on my numb lil feet, ok … I am not really, as if I were, I would be as stable as a weeble!

Dr I was confident that after treatment number 4 I would have had enough of the devil drug to do the job so treatment 5 was a bonus.

Unfortunately, this does not mean the end of chemo but while the Capecitabine tablets are unpleasant, comparing them with the Oxaliplatin is a bit like comparing Smarties with Snail Bait. It is incredible how one's perspective on bad changes when exposed to a whole new level of bad!! So, I will continue to take the tablets until April but hopefully a certain level of normality can resume as soon as I am back on my feet. This potentially means that as soon as a few weeks I can get back to work. My goal now is to get my body strong enough to ensure it can fight off any nasties that try set up camp again.

It is proven that being fit reduces the likelihood of a recurrence by 50%, these are good odds so time to get my ass in gear. This new fitness plan will be done with the support of my ex D aka Grumpy who is currently studying to become a Personal Trainer. Interesting point this, after two years of torture and misery I now voluntarily put myself at the mercy of somebody with whom I have the shared experience of a divorce …. maybe I is not so clever as everybody thinks I is? Just kidding, I have every faith in Duncan and while I am sure there will be times when kettlebells will fly (ok, almost fly – I have to pick them up first) I know that he will make sure I am fighting fit in no time. So hopefully soon I will come out of seclusion and be able to see all of you and not just talk at you through my blog. Happy day

Chapter 36

The frustration of feeling useless

I find myself again sitting fuming at the sheer frustration of my position. This time however is not due to the side effects, feeling shit is normal for me now. My frustration is at being useless, like TOTALLY useless. As you are all aware we move house next week, before I could have been whizzing around for hours getting stuff sorted, now I can manage at best 30 minutes of light labour which invariably ends up with me sitting on the settee praying that I won't end up projectile vomiting my porridge across the room and shaking like a jelly (I said jelly and not leaf as I am definitely more jelly like in consistency).

This more than anything brings on the toddler like tantrums, I hate relying on everybody to do everything for me, I am the Mum of the house, I want to fulfil my role as Mum but spend most of my time watching everyone else doing Mum things while I sit nursing my stupid hands and feet. Aaaaaaaargh!!!!

I so often wonder if my family don't secretly get frustrated with me as well? How would I feel to get home and the dishwasher hasn't been unpacked and the washing is untouched? (these chores scare me as these are "cold" chores and the hands don't like them.) Would I be forgiving and understanding, or would I get hacked off with the lump on the settee with the "poor little me" face? I like to believe I would but after 4 months of it would I be tempted to beat the lump over the head with the griddle pan (after having to take it out of the dishwasher because lump ignored it all day!)

Before any of you stage an intervention, there is no indication that my loved one's are conspiring to put me (and themselves) out of my misery once and for all, I simply wonder how I would feel in their shoes.

Chapter 37

A few glorious days where cancer hardly existed.

We did it, we moved into our beautiful new home. Well truth be told I sat and watched as an amazing crew made up of friends and family moved all my worldly belongings from one side of the village to another in what can only be described as blizzard conditions.

Not only did they help us move but my mother-in-law, brother-in-law and sister-in-law deep cleaned the old house until it sparkled, don't think it has ever been so clean! How incredibly fortunate are we to have these people in our lives.

Naturally with me being a little slow and not very useful the unpacking side of things is a little slow to say the least. I have sat and given a lot of instructions; my Nades spent all day on Friday moving items from cupboard to cupboard in the kitchen as I kept changing my mind on where things should go. Love you Nades, thank you for tolerating my cupboard commitment issues.

To explain the title of this post despite being slow and having sore and somewhat unstable feet (will suddenly start falling over as feet lose sensation, rather amusing for anybody watching) therefore having to rely heavily on others to do the heavy lifting the past few days have been glorious, my focus has been on my home and not on the hideous curse that is cancer and the treatment thereof, there were brief moments I didn't think about it at all. Sheer bliss!

I can only hope that there will be more of these moments in the future, and these moments will become more frequent and the duration of said moments becoming longer. To be mentally free from the darkness is like a much-needed holiday.

This Saturday will be the 1-year anniversary of my diagnosis, a whole year since the condition that plagued me was given a name, and it was the last name I wanted to hear. However, I have survived the worst of it (we hope) and I do believe that I have come through this wiser than I was before. I know what is important now and what is simply noise. I hold my loved ones closer and relish the time I spend with them.

Chapter 38

Back to reality

The day has come, the day I return my sorry self-back to the world. I start work again tomorrow, in agreement with the all-knowing medical professionals I will only be going back part time while still on treatment as if I try to pull a full shift the following things are going to happen:

- I will fall asleep at my desk at approximately 13h00 which is the time the drugs generally cause me to become narcoleptic.

- I will run my already frail immune system into the ground and end up back in my sick bed, God forbid.

- If I have not left the building by 12h30 Steve will wag his finger at me and give me that stern look filled with deep disapproval. This look makes the dog who weighs 60kg and can snap a frozen chicken drumstick with little to no effort hide away in fear so don't fancy me fairing to well …

I am excited to be going back, I wish I felt better, my hands and feet are still causing me grief and nausea remains my constant companion. But it is time, my brain is slowly dying because of too much daytime telly and if I must hobble around for 4 hours clutching my anti puke drugs then so be it.

I would be lying if I said I wasn't a little apprehensive, what if I can't cope, what if my chemo brain causes me to make a colossal cock up or worse, say something wholly inappropriate due to my inner filter being compromised by my partially functioning mind? In HR this is a no-no and while I don't really fit the typical mould of an HR professional anyway, I have taught myself to "shut it" when the situation commands as much but fear this skill may be lost to me after all this time.

Keep fingers crossed for me folks, this could all go horribly wrong?! As for the cancer/chemo stuff all is chugging along as it should be, on cycle 7 now with only 1 more to go. I see a HUGE celebration in about 6 weeks. The end of the nightmare year and hopefully the end of my cancer story. Well best get some shut eye as sleep deprivation combined with chemo brain could most definitely bring about the end of my career.

Chapter 39

Who and where am I?

This post is not directly about cancer, treatment or side effects but as a place for me to get my thoughts in order as for some reason I feel confused, out of place in my space as such. I find I do this best when putting words to paper so here we go.

An odd thing seems to have happened to me, it seems when you are removed from the real world for an extended period you find yourself wondering if the time you have lost has somehow made you lose your place, like stepping out of the queue at the supermarket and having to go all the way to the back of the line again.

Do I feel this way because I have changed due to my experiences over the past year and no longer fit neatly back into my original slot or is it because when you are removed for a while you see things with fresh eyes, eyes that cannot avoid seeing situations clearly, seeing things for what they are and not what over time convinced yourself they were?

The world around me seems cruel, full of blame, people no longer care about each other but seem intent on destroying each other to elevate themselves or safeguard their current position. Was it always this way but I didn't see it? I look back and see that much to my shame I was a part of this game, I played it with the same ferocity as those I stand back and look upon with horror. I am ashamed but hopeful that this clarity will afford me the chance to do better.

Cancer has taught me that there are bigger enemies out there than each other, we need to be kinder and conduct ourselves with honour and instead of seeing an opportunity for growth on the back of a troubled soul, see it as a chance to extend a hand offering aid when most needed. One of my favourite sayings is "One day I hope to become the person my dog thinks I am", I think this needs to become my life plan so I can become someone I am proud of.

Any of you with me?

Chapter 40

The sun is shining again

Today was a good day, ok, I slept through most of it but the bits I saw were marvellous. I have crawled out of the slump I was in; I have made peace with where my life is at. I need to vent to get the poison out of my system to move past it and I did, but I apologise that you all had to listen to me whine, yet again.

Physically I am not up to much now and probably sleep for about 16 hours of the 24 given per day, one thing I will try to do every day is take Dave the dog out for a walk. It is not very comfortable as my feet smart now but overall; I generally feel better for it.

We are virtually in the countryside so have some glorious walks nearby, one of which takes us along a brook where fuzz nugget likes to swim, as you can imagine being a 9-stone hound of which I reckon 3 stone is fur alone can be quite uncomfortable in this heat so he is quite partial to a dip.

As I sat and watched him paddling around (which is a joy to watch) it occurred to me that I am generally so lucky, again if we ignore the annoying cancer bit I have a wonderful life and to allow negative thoughts and feelings cloud any part of my life will only see me losing out. This journey is full of ups and downs and I don't expect this to be my last down. I get angry so much quicker (and I was volatile before all this so not good), the Oncologist did warn me about this from the start … I wonder if there is brandy in this stuff as that has the same effect on me … hhmmmm?!)

The best news is I only have 6 days to go, hooray! That is only 48 tablets left out of 1,316 being the total number prescribed at the beginning of last year. I so got this! And to top it off my final week is turning out to be the most beautiful of the year so far., thank you mother nature! Thank you all for your support and words of encouragement when I get low, your understanding and words of wisdom see me through some dark times.

Chapter 41

Done & dusted

And we are done folks! I (hopefully) took my last ever chemo this evening. The anticipated joy I expected to feel at this moment doesn't even come close to how happy I am right now. It has been a LONG year, there have been a few highs and many lows, the lowest being this past weekend when my youngest son ripped his hand open in a mud run, I say ripped as his hand looked like he had been mauled by a small shark. He had to endure many painful procedures to sort it out including surgery.

While it had nothing to do with cancer/chemo it was excruciatingly painful for him and as mentioned in a previous post anything happens to my children, I end up a blubbering mess. I have been a pathetic wreck for the past few days. He was so brave considering and has even campaigned to return to school tomorrow as it seems the boredom is more painful than the hand.

As for me while the treatment is over, I know my journey is not. My body has been put through the mill and needs a lot of TLC before it will forgive me for the past year. But the main thing is in a week or so I should feel like a different person and should hopefully return to society as a semi productive body.

Lessons learnt:

- I am not invincible, there are things bigger, stronger and uglier than me which I cannot control and need to stop trying … let's call this one a work in progress.

- Tomorrow is never guaranteed, enjoy the things that are important today.

- The value of good friends, there are people who have been so incredibly supportive, they have given up their own time to be there for me. I will love you all forever and will never take you for granted.

- Listen to your body and don't be afraid to push for further investigation if you suspect there is something wrong, the earlier this beast is caught the better your chance of beating it.

Sadly, as I end this phase of my journey with this dreadful disease a beloved family member starts theirs. They are in my thoughts and prayers and my hope is they too beat this monster and that the treatment is kind. We are all rooting for you!

We now begin the waiting game, I will have annual check-ups for the next 5 years, I would be lying if I said I wasn't anxious but those who have gone before me have said as the years pass the dark cloud of cancer passes and eventually becomes just wisps against a bright blue sky. Here's hoping I can be one of those who gets to celebrate the 5 years all clear. Thank you to all of you who have been there for myself and my family through all of this, even just knowing that you were listening to me whinging made me feel better (a problem shared and all that!)

I've got Cancer where?

Chapter 42

Keeping busy … avoidance tactic perhaps?

My life suddenly became super busy, I found myself in a place where there was no time in my day that was not full. I get up at 5:30am to go to gym, rush back home to get ready for work. I then dash into the office and am busy, busy, busy all day. At 5pm I leave work, get home, walk Dave, do dinner. Sit down, open my laptop and continue to work until about 11pm, go to sleep to wake up and start again.

I was lying here thinking how crazy things have been and had an epiphany, yes, work is manic right now, but it has been before so why do I feel I now need to conquer the world overnight? And then it hit me … I got a letter 3 weeks ago informing me that I needed to go for blood tests in preparation for my first-year scan in October.

To avoid the feeling of terror taking hold because the moment we find out if I remain free of disease or not has arrived, I turned into the equivalent of the energiser bunny on speed. I needed to fill every space so there was no time to think.

I know there is a chance the bastard disease may still be somewhere in there. Every pain, twitch or itch inside sends my brain into overdrive. I know the chance of recurrence is high, and despite doing everything I can to avoid it, the outcome is ultimately out of my hands.

When people ask how I am doing and what happens next for me, the stock response they give to my telling them about my one-year check-up is "think positive and you will be fine!" My spoken response is, "absolutely!" The unspoken response is, "WTF! If it were that bloody simple the pharmaceutical companies would go bust!"

As much as I am a believer in the power of positive thinking, I am not sure that I possess a mental strength powerful enough to destroy one of the deadliest diseases mankind faces! I think I need to start small, maybe I'll try bending a spoon with my mind first … The time draws near and there is no avoiding it, the scan will happen, and the news will be good or not. I don't believe there is anything I can do to prepare myself for the scenario where the news is bad. What will be will be.

Time to go to sleep to prepare for another busy day of thought avoidance!

Chapter 43

Scanxiety … it's real folks!

Still no word on a scan date yet, part of me just wants it over but most of me would rather just avoid it altogether. I am tempted when receiving the results to just stick my fingers in my ears and go "la la la" until the messenger stops speaking, I just don't want to play this game anymore, it sucks! I continue to need to keep busy as this is all that is preserving my sanity.

The latest project, I decided that I NEEDED a dressing room, I am the least girliest girl EVER, this is like giving a toffee to a man with no teeth, nice idea but pointless!

Glamour for me is putting on mascara and donning shoes with heels no higher than an inch, any higher and I am going to do an ankle. But this fact was totally unimportant as this exercise became an obsession.

Steve and his wonderful brother accommodated my whim and bravely hauled the heaviest dresser up our rather awkward stairs for me, my dear brother-in-law injuring his back in the process.

Sorry again Aaron. I then spent the weekend sorting all my clothes in order, coats, jackets, long sleeve t-shirts, short sleeve t-shirts, work blouses, smart trousers, casual trousers, skirts then dresses.

All had to be on matching coat hangers as the prospect of a lone wooden hanger among my velvet flocked hangers almost required the use of a brown paper bag! I would continue to tell you about the arrangement of the socks however I think from the above you get the idea.

When Project Dressing Room was over the panic set in … so … every cupboard in the house was fair game!

My long-suffering family stood by and watched as I flew around like a whirling dervish! The mind is cruel and irrational at the best of times but mine is utterly ridiculous! Every time I look in the mirror I am convinced I look close to death, I am convinced that every time my skin itches it is a clear sign the cancer is in my liver (common sense is rolling her eyes saying, "it is getting colder love, try using some of that body lotion that is currently artistically positioned on your dressing table for its intended use and not just stood there for effect, doing so may solve this particular problem!"

I look at my face and panic because it looks different, thinner, this must be cancer related! Again, common sense is sarcastically suggesting that my current regime of a calorie restricted diet along with an intense morning workout at the gym is likely to result in this outcome as I am losing weight (as is the intention of this sudden lifestyle change) but it is freaking me out, there is just no pleasing some people!

I am finding something rather refreshing in my current mind set, I am a massive people pleaser, I would rather deliberately avoid a conversation or simply say what the person wants to hear rather than tell a truth that may offend or hurt, (not proud of the fact that I am a complete chicken shit but hey ho!). However, no more me duck! I have no brain space available for niceties, if I thinks it, I says it ... simples!

After delivering a presentation to a group of new Board Directors last week when asked a direct question on a rather sensitive area, I shared my thoughts without hesitation not really considering any potential repercussions from being rather forthright, a dear colleague and friend said to me afterwards something along the lines of, "don't ask a Survivor for honesty unless you really want the truth as that's what you will get!" I suppose considering my new approach it is probably best I get this scan over with as it could become rather career limiting!

I am terrified, there is no other way to put it. I am walking around in a constant state of fear, there is no denying it. I am not scared of death, I am scared of the prospect of having to go through chemo again, it was a hell I remain mentally scarred from. Time to sleep, praying for dreams filled with puppies and sunshine.

I've got Cancer where?

Chapter 44

Time to live!

I eventually got my letter, my scan was set for Sunday the 24th November, this was my first husband A's birthday, I had to see this as a good sign. I felt he was sending me a message telling me that everything was going to be alright. That he was watching over me. Scan day arrived, the whole family came along for support and waited until I was done. Then it was time to wait.

Unfortunately, I had to wait until after the New Year for the results, when they arrived I would love to add for dramatic effect that I held the letter with shaking hands and a deep sense of trepidation. I didn't, I am a simple soul and not good at waiting … for anything! I ripped open the letter and there they were, the words everybody who has gone through this wants to read in the report, **NO EVIDENCE OF DISEASE.**

I had made it, 1 year free of recurrence, the relief is indescribable.

At that point I made a decision, my cancer experience was now going to be a thing that lives in my past, I will no longer allow it to cloud my every thought. So this brings this blog to a natural conclusion, as to continue means I am still allowing Cancer in, allowing it to be a part of my thoughts, to continue to let it be an important feature of my life. I am no longer afraid of dying, I am afraid of not living, to some extent there are the same words however they have a vastly different meaning. We go through life being careful, not taking risks afraid of getting hurt. I intend to take every opportunity offered to do everything I have ever wanted to do.

I have always dreamed of getting my motorbike licence and travelling to far flung parts of the globe on two wheels. This always seemed like a fantasy, too farfetched for me to even contemplate. However, before my 50th birthday which will mark the year of my 5 year all clear I intend to do a two-week solo trip, why many ask? Why not I say. This entry is short and sweet and probably not a perfect ending, but like I said, I am no writer and I don't know the rules of ending something like this. Thank you all for reading, I bid you farewell and appreciate all the love and support shown to me during all of this.

Chapter 45

Two years on …

I decided to read my blog again after avoiding it for the past year as the memories were not comfortable ones. The reason for this was motivated by receiving a friend request on Facebook from my first ever high school crush, Brendan. On accepting the friend request, I did what all self-respecting women do, enter full on social media stalking mode! Unfortunately, one of the first posts I found showed a photo of him having his first round of Chemo after receiving a diagnosis of Stage 4 Lung Cancer. I don't know why this had such a profound effect on me, but it did.

When looking further, I discovered that he had not long been married to a woman who quite clearly adored him, and he quite obviously felt the same. This made me sad, angry and raging against the injustice of it all. Two people who found each other, loved each other and should be spending the rest of their lives together now face the possibility that the future they had planned now hangs in the balance. I really hate this bloody disease!

Brendan, if I were religious, I would pray for you, however I am not so all I can offer is my thoughts for you and your lovely lady during this difficult time. And to say thank you for tolerating 13-year-old me making ridiculous puppy eyes at you!

SO much has changed, so after 11 years at my job, I left. I decided one day that the role, company no longer served me. I wanted something different so left and am now doing a role for significantly less money but have not been this happy and fulfilled in a job for a long time.

Another change, Steve and I are no longer a couple, however we remain good friends and I am delighted to say Steve has met a wonderful lady, Louise who as embraced the relationship Steve and I have and has become a very important part of the equation. Steve has even on occasion invited me to go out riding with him to give me some practice, him on his gorgeous Kawasaki Vulcan and me wobbling behind on my ridiculous little red Honda CBF 125cc.

Yes, the plan to be a badass biker chick is well underway. Ok, maybe not well underway but I can actually stay upright, turn a corner and have only dropped my bike once … at a standstill, I mean who knew parking on an uneven surface was a bad idea?

So, within this past year, I have met a wonderful woman who started out as a neighbour and a friend, but someone who I realised after a while was so much more. Enter Sarah! Yup, I fell in love with a woman. Again, one of the lessons the past few years has taught me, don't miss a chance at happiness, whatever form it takes. In this case it was finding that person who loves the things I love, who shares the same values as me and loves me, my gorgeous child and the chunk muffin despite the chaos we have brought into her world. She is beautiful, brilliant and makes me laugh until my sides hurt. And she has said I can go to the US next year to do a solo bike trip, the only condition given was that I had to remember to take photos, something I am not great at doing!

We have already made some wonderful memories as a couple and as a family. The most recent being a dive trip to the Maldives where after thousands of dives, I finally got to see and be beaten about the face by the illusive Manta Ray. I look forward to many more adventures (that do not involve climbing up a bloody mountain in Scotland that nigh on killed me!)

I think my 14 year old is extremely grateful that Sarah has come into our lives as they talk politics, poetry and famous works of literature, while I sit in the same room repeatedly calling them nerds and referring to the conversation as BORING!   Jokes aside, I am extremely proud of what a beautiful, brilliant, confident and interesting person my youngest is growing up to be.   You will remember at the beginning of this blog, I suspected this child was going to be just like his mother, I am pleased to report that for the most part the only characteristics we share is a strong opinion and a healthy dose of self-confidence.   Thanks to the wonders of modern medicine, I so look forward to seeing the superb adult this child is going to be.

Life is good, I am grateful to still be here and to have been given the opportunity to do and see all the things that for a moment I was convinced were never going to happen.

I refer back to my English teacher who told me that I never ended my essays very well, so in her honour, that folks, I finish this book by saying...

Book finished!

Printed by Amazon Italia Logistica S.r.l.
Torrazza Piemonte (TO), Italy

13359621R00096